JUSTICE AND THE LEGAL
SYSTEM IN THE U.S.S.R.

THE CONTEMPORARY SOVIET UNION SERIES:
INSTITUTIONS AND POLICIES

Each volume in the Contemporary Soviet Union Series examines in detail the facts about an important aspect of Soviet rule as it has affected the Soviet citizen in the 50 years since the Bolshevik Revolution of 1917.

Subjects include industry, culture, religion, agriculture, and so on. A careful examination of official Soviet material in each field provides essential basic reading for all students of Soviet affairs.

Robert Conquest is a former Research Fellow in Soviet affairs at the London School of Economics and Political Science and Senior Fellow of Columbia University's Russian Institute. His works include *Power and Policy in the U.S.S.R.*, *The Pasternak Affair: Courage of Genius*, *Common Sense About Russia*, *The Soviet Deportation of Nationalities*, and *Russia after Khrushchev*.

THE CONTEMPORARY SOVIET UNION SERIES:
INSTITUTIONS AND POLICIES
EDITED BY ROBERT CONQUEST

Justice and the Legal System in the U.S.S.R.

FREDERICK A. PRAEGER, *Publishers*
New York · Washington

BOOKS THAT MATTER

Published in the United States of America in 1968
by Frederick A. Praeger, Inc., Publishers
111 Fourth Avenue, New York, N.Y. 10003

Introduction © 1968 in London, England, by Robert
Conquest

All rights reserved

Library of Congress Catalog Card Number: 68-26181

Printed in Great Britain

Contents

Editor's Preface

In this book, while indicating the limitations and difficulties surrounding the legal profession and legal system in the USSR, our main concern is to give a clear theoretical and practical account of the machinery and principles of Soviet law. The other side of the picture—the great police machine which has constituted the apparatus of illegality and State intrusion—is dealt with in a companion volume, *The Soviet Police System*.

In 1956, after the XXth Congress of the Communist Party of the Soviet Union, the Italian Left-wing Socialist leader Pietro Nenni wrote confidentially to Mikhail Suslov, ideological Secretary of the Central Committee. He said that the denunciation of Stalin's methods which had just been made called in question the whole 'juridical and political structure of the State'; and he noted that the fault of the earlier period had lain not so much in Stalin's or Beria's personal tendencies as in 'the absence of any system of juridical guarantees against abuses of power'.*

The work of the present 'liberal' lawyers in the Soviet Union in trying to fully institutionalise the law is sound in principle. But it may be doubted whether it can prove a bulwark against a resurgence of State illegality, unless the political structure is likewise altered to the degree of institutionalising the whole basis of the rule of law. The problem in fact goes deeper than specific codification, to the very nature of the State.

Marx envisaged, in the interim 'Socialist' period between 'Capitalism' and 'Communism', specific social and economic measures to be enforced by the proletarian State, and hence a system of regulations. On the other hand, he expected the period to be a short one, and often treats it as a sort of emergency government by decree, giving some basis to the idea of political tribunals relying on class instinct rather than specific law which was common in the early Soviet period.

* *Avanti*, October 25, 1964.

[7]

The first years of the Soviet régime held the country under what amounted to martial law in all fields, including the economic. By and large legality was simply what the Party did—though, of course, its lower organs could be overruled by the centre. The criterion was simply whether an action was consonant with Party policy or with the strategy of the Civil War.

When it became clear that the 'Socialist' period was going to be a long one, a certain stabilisation set in. Pure arbitrariness is a poor basis for any society over any but the shortest period. A demand immediately arises for clarity and definition of the regulations, so that the relevant relationships can be properly established. Lawyers (though not all lawyers) were naturally prominent in seeking this sort of stability in the Soviet Union. The school opposed to them cited, and cites, the overriding rights of the State. Even at present there is no question, indeed, of opposing these rights in principle, and the controversy is fought out rather on the ground of establishing as large an area as possible in which legality can prevail.

From early days, the Police had openly conducted not only the investigative, but also, in many cases, the 'judicial' aspect of political cases. In March, 1920, the Cheka was authorised to sentence people to up to five years in labour camps by administrative decision if the investigation did not 'reveal sufficient evidence' for judicial proceedings.* We have the Cheka archives from Smolensk covering the period February–April 1921, which give the minutes of many cases, including sentences.† There is no reference to any law on which decisions are based, the accused are absent, and there is no record of any defence.

By a curious irony, the victory of the codifiers over the adherents of loose revolutionary tribunals came with the Great Purge. Vyshinsky, the central figure of Stalin's legal system, officially favoured codification as against the open assertion of State pragmatism on the part of his academic opponents of the early 'Thirties (who all perished as a result). The great public trials of 1936–38 were, of course, complete falsifications. But they were conducted with much attention to both legal and procedural considerations.

* RSFSR *Laws*, 1920–22,23:115.
† Simon Wolin and Robert M. Slusser, *The Soviet Secret Police*, *New York*, 1957, *pp.* 36–7.

[8]

However, the appearances were on the whole kept up in proportion to the desire to make a public impression. In principle, Vyshinsky ruled that 'When it is a question of annihilating the enemy, we can do it just as well without a trial.'* There was a range of quasi-judicial bodies, from the strictly legal Military Collegium of the Supreme Court, through the Special Board of the NKVD, which had at least a semblance of legalisation through a public founding decree, to the *Troikas* instituted in the provinces in about August 1937, which had no known authorisation whatever.

The Special Board was specifically empowered to deal with those against whom there was insufficient evidence for the Courts. The categories under which they were sentenced included such extraordinary crimes as 'suspicion of espionage'. There were in addition categories such as 'Socially Dangerous Element'—often the children or other relatives of purgees— who could be exiled without even a Special Board 'trial', by decision of the Prosecutor.

It would be a mistake, however, to suppose that greater equity or humanity was to be found in the formally constituted bodies. For Vyshinsky was in effect incorporating into the forms of legality the substance of arbitrariness. He issued instructions that 'probability of guilt was adequate for sentence', and that this could be detected by 'political flair' rather than evidence.* Sentences were prepared in advance in cases before the Military Collegium,† and in other court cases.‡

In recent years Vyshinsky's more extravagant excesses have been denounced. For example, his insistence on confession as the best sort of evidence has been severely criticised in the Soviet legal press. Nevertheless, it remains the aim in important cases. It was required, for example, of Penkovsky and Wynne. And where confession has not been in fact obtained, as in the Bukovsky trial, the official reports have nevertheless stated the opposite. In general, the progress made by advocates of true legality has been important but not decisive.

The general feeling that the trials of Brooke, Sinyavsky and Daniel, Bukovsky, Galanskov and Ginsburg, and many others,

* *Sovetskoye Gosudarstvo i Pravo*, No. 3, 1965.

† Khrushchev: Confidential Report to the XX Congress of the CPSU.

‡ Shelepin: Speech to the XXII Congress of the CPSU.

are operations of the KGB rather than normal judicial procedures has lately been strengthened by a number of developments. One of these was the extraordinary action of the Supreme Soviet in approving the addition to the Supreme Court of two prominent members of the KGB itself, an act unprecedented even in Stalin's time: the composition of that Court, as approved in October 1967,* includes as Vice-Chairman S. G. Bannikov, Head of the KGB in Turkmenia from 1956 to 1963, and after that Vice-Chairman of the USSR KGB; while N. F. Chistyakov, former Senior Investigator in the KGB with the rank of Major-General of State Security, is now a member of the Court and Chairman of its Military Collegium.

Again, there has been an increased reliance on laws which are in contradiction to basic legislation, and are not commonly available to the public, as in certain recent religious cases. Similarly, we find that foreign journalists were forbidden to interview Mrs Ginsburg and Mrs Galanskov, on January 18, 1968, on the basis of a dubious "administrative" requirement, dating from 1947, in their formal accreditations.

It is true that even a *Rechtstaat* may have inequitable laws. Codification, even accompanied by exemplary interpretation of the code, does not in itself mean justice—for the laws themselves may be unjust. (In this connection it is perhaps worth noting that Soviet criminal law, better codified than the civic or political equivalents, is by Western standards remarkably backward in its penal provisions: see especially p. 80 below, on the death penalty.) But if codification is not a sufficient condition for equity, it is nevertheless a necessary condition. And the mere submission by the executive to the concept of legality tends to go with the abandonment of absolutist and dictatorial claims for the State, and thus implies, at one remove, a tendency to liberalise the laws themselves.

Meanwhile, so long as the Soviet state maintains its right to override, not merely in extreme emergencies but in all cases where its interests are felt to be involved, the letter and spirit of its own laws, advances towards general legality have no guarantee of permanence. The past three years have seen a notable increase in Police and State intervention and abuse of the law. Future developments must depend on political and

* *Pravda*, October 14, 1967.

civic factors of which the legal controversy is no more than a single aspect. Nevertheless, it is in the domain of the law, whose history, principles and organisation are here set forth, that changes, good or bad, will be finally formalised.

Thanks for invaluable collaboration are due in the first place to A. Alexeyenko; to H. S. Murray; and to L. Levine, who drew my attention to much fresh material.

ROBERT CONQUEST

I

Development of the
Soviet Legal and Judicial System

One of the first acts of the Soviet authorities on coming to power was to abolish the pre-revolutionary judicial and legal system. A decree of November 24, 1917, swept away all former courts and laid down that the new courts were to be guided by former laws

'only in so far as these have not been annulled by the Revolution and are not in contradiction with revolutionary conscience and the revolutionary concept of justice.'[1]

This was not achieved without difficulty—the existing judicial bodies refused to recognise the validity of the decree and, for instance, Red Army troops had to be used to put a stop to the functioning of the existing courts in Moscow;[2] what proved far more difficult, however, both then and for the next two decades, was the formation of the Soviet attitude towards law in general.

Marx and Engels had viewed law as merely part of the superstructure of society, the content, purpose and very existence of which was determined by the economic basis. Law was thus an instrument by means of which the ruling class kept itself in power; though its content might change in accordance with the economic relations peculiar to any given capitalist society, it drew its *raison d'être* from the existence of divided and antagonistic classes. It was expected that with the triumph of Communism a classless society would be achieved and that this must involve the withering away of the State and the disappearance of its handmaiden—law. The choice was, therefore, not between bourgeois law and Socialist law, but between law as such and a new social order based on administration. As Stuchka, Chairman of the Supreme Court, wrote in 1927:

'Communism means not the victory of Socialist laws but the victory of Socialism over any law, since, with the abolition of classes with their economic interests, law will disappear altogether.'[3]

[13]

Several of the earliest decrees of the Bolshevik Government were of a purely declaratory nature. Even those creating judicial institutions and procedures were cast in a general, permissive form. The Revolutionary Tribunals which, with the Cheka, were effectively the dominant organ for the administration of justice, were declared to be free from any limitations, save in those cases where a minimum punishment had been stipulated.[4] Until November, 1918, any citizen could act as a prosecutor and up to March, 1918, as defence counsel.[5]

In the state of emergency then prevailing it was hardly surprising that the bulk of normative acts produced dealt with such matters as counter-revolution, desertion and speculation. Civil litigation was at a discount and the message of the Leading Principles of Criminal Law, worked out in 1919 by the People's Commissariat, was that:

'In the interests of economising forces and co-ordinating and centralising unco-ordinated action, the proletariat ought to work out rules for curbing its class enemies, ought to create a method of struggle with its enemies and to learn to dominate them. And first of all this ought to relate to criminal law, which has as its task the struggle against the violators of the new conditions of community life that are taking shape in the transitional period of the dictatorship of the proletariat. Only with the final smashing of the resistance of the overthrown bourgeois and intermediate classes and the realisation of a Communist order will the proletariat annihilate both the State as an organisation of coercion, and law as a function of the State.'[6]

Private ownership of land and the means of production were abolished, along with inheritance and private trade in consumer goods. But the period of 'War Communism' was not then conceived of as being merely, or even mainly, one of destruction. The seeds of the practical and imminent realisation of Socialism were deemed to lie in the distribution of commodities by ration cards, the payment of wages partially in kind, and the elimination of monetary transactions as between State agencies. But the legal codes produced during the period 1917–21 were of a fragmentary, transitional nature, more concerned with abolishing past norms than with introducing new ones. The Family Code of October, 1918,[7] freed marriage and divorce from Church control and the Labour Code of December, 1918,[8] did little more than protect workers in the employ-

ment of such private owners as remained against the time
when the latter would cease to exist.

1921–28 THE NEW ECONOMIC POLICY

However, the expectation of world revolution did not material-
ise and a postponement of the transition to a classless society
inside the USSR, regulated not by law but by voluntary economic relationships, became necessary. The period of the New
Economic Policy (1921–28) was intended to provide an economic breathing space; in law it was a period of considerable
activity. In 1922 and 1923 a new Judiciary Act,[9] a Civil Code,[10]
a Code of Criminal Procedure,[11] a Criminal Code,[12] a Land
Code[13] and a new Labour Code[14] all made their appearance.
The first Corrective Labour Code was enacted in 1924.[15] The
Family Code of 1918 was redrafted in 1926,[16] and the 1922
Criminal Code likewise in the same year.[17] This spate of codification outwardly marked a sharp break with the attitude towards law and the State characteristic of the period of War
Communism—it was largely formulated on the lines of bourgeois law. Yet there were certain significant innovations; in
civil law it was provided that any legal transaction 'directed to
the obvious prejudice of the State' should be invalid and that
any consequent profits should be forfeit to the State as 'unjust
enrichment'; in criminal law the doctrine of analogy was
devised,*[18] and the notion of 'social danger' bulked large as a
criterion of justice. All this, however, did not amount to an
ideological retreat. It was not then admitted that the withering
away of State and law had been postponed to the Greek
Kalends. Rather was it that in the transitional period law was
considered a handier and more efficient weapon than unregu-
lated coercion for the preservation of the proletarian dictatorship at that stage, and for the preparation for a move forward
to a classless society. Law could help to pave the way to its
own elimination.

1928–36 THE BIRTH OF STALINISM

The NEP period gave way to the era of forced collectivisation
and industrialisation. Under War Communism the main task
had been the preservation of the régime from its opponents;

* *See* page 138.

[15]

under NEP the strict delimitation of the activities of private traders; from 1931 it was the protection and strengthening of the economic programme which governed the utilisation of law in the Soviet Union. Though the exponents of what came subsequently to be called the 'nihilist attitude to law'[19] (among them the People's Commissar for Justice up to 1937, Krylenko) continued very much in evidence until 1934 and were not finally denounced and disgraced until 1937, the writing on the wall was already there. As early as 1929 Stalin warned:

'The anarchist theory of "blowing up the State" must not be confused with the Marxist theory of "breaking-up", "smashing" the bourgeois State machine. Lenin . . . criticised and demolished the anarchist theory, and proposed in its place the theory of a new State of proletarian dictatorship.'[20]

At the same time the legal 'nihilists' also modified their position: they accepted the strengthening of the State, but were against any concomitant strengthening of the legal system. Their answer to the situation in which total planning rendered obsolete a lot of NEP legislation was that planning must replace law and social-economic policy determine the enactment of regulatory norms. As the leader of this school of thought wrote in 1930:

'The relationship of law to politics and to economics is utterly different among us from what it is in bourgeois society . . . In bourgeois-capitalist society, the legal superstructure should have maximum immobility—maximum stability—because it represents a firm framework of the movement of the economic forces whose bearers are capitalist *entrepreneurs* . . . Among us it is different. We require that our legislation possess maximum elasticity. We cannot fetter ourselves by any sort of system . . . Accordingly, at a time when bourgeois political scientists are striving to depict politics itself as law—to dissolve politics in law—law occupies among us, on the contrary, a subordinate position with reference to politics. We have a system of proletarian politics, but we have no need for any sort of juridical system of proletarian law. We have a system of proletarian politics and upon it law should be orientated. Once we even wished to arrange the curriculum so that, for example, the course in land law would be replaced by a course in land policy and law, because among us law can play no independent and final part: this was the design when War Communism was going out. During the years of the New Economic Policy and of the rehabilitation period, the system of codes was introduced and began again to develop, and at the same time attempts to pack and to tie all law into a system were renewed. Now, when we have passed to the

[16]

reconstruction period, the utmost dynamic force is essential . . .
Revolutionary legality is for us a problem which is 99 per cent
political.'[21]

Five years later Vyshinsky wrote:

'The formal law is subordinate to the law of the Revolution.
There might be collisions and discrepancies between the formal
commands of laws and those of the proletarian revolution . . . This
collision must be solved only by the subordination of the formal
commands of law to those of Party policy.'[22]

Neither of these statements was viewed as being incompat-
ible with Stalin's pronouncement that the Bolsheviks stood for
the strengthening of the dictatorship of the proletariat as the
prelude to the withering away of Government power.[23] It was
agreed that compliance with norms set up by an external body
(the State) was not law; that law was only one of the possible
means of social control. In consequence, the legislation of the
early '30s was marked by its emphasis on discretionary powers,
on coercive effect, and on its direct reflection of State policy.
Civil law was largely neglected, and the drafts of the new
criminal codes appearing between 1930 and 1935 minimised
the element of personal guilt and evaluated crime in terms of
the social character, social background and social intent of the
offender. In the field of legal theory, as has been stated, one
consequence was that

'from about 1929 until 1937 there were scarcely any works in
journals or in monograph form dealing with the problems of the
concept of *corpus delicti*, the formulation of the legal criteria of
crime, and current criminal legislation likewise was virtually un-
subjected to critical analysis from the standpoint of the need to
establish in it precise criteria of various institutes of criminal law
and *corpora delicti*.'[24]

Bearing in mind that this was the era of the mass liquidation
of the *kulaks*, of the systematic introduction of police controls
and of the effective stifling of oppositional trends among the
trade unions, the then prevailing theory of, as it were, the
pragmatic exploitation of law contributed in no small degree
to removing such barriers to coercive repression as still existed.

1936 AND AFTER: THE CONSOLIDATION OF STALINISM

Yet the premises from which legal pragmatism had sprung
depended for their fulfilment not only upon the emergence of a

classless society but upon the doctrinal recognition of such emergence. In 1933 Stalin had added a new postulate to his earlier statements about the withering away of the State, linking it with the 'organisation of defence against capital encirclement which is as yet far from being, and will not soon be, destroyed'.[25] In 1936, when the new Constitution was in the final stage of drafting, it was stated that a Socialist society had been achieved in the USSR; the first phase of Communism—Socialism—realised; that 'antagonistic' classes no longer existed in the USSR, only 'friendly' ones.[26] Yet not only was there then to be no withering away of State and law, but the existence of a (classless) State and a (classless) law became to be regarded not as a necessary and temporary evil but as a positive and continuing good. Moreover, the postulate of the liquidation of capitalist encirclement was expanded by Stalin in 1939 to be a factor governing the possibility of the withering away of the State even in the final stage of Communism.[27]

Against the ideological background of the departure from Marxism, the post-1936 period saw the gradual rout of those theories which had been erected on the basis of the Marxist negation of law. At the same time as the institutional pattern was established, family relationships formally recognised, the Church allotted a restricted but specified rôle in Soviet life, economic incentives and differentials introduced, and personal property regularised, a system of Socialist law had to be devised. The main spokesman for this new drive towards legal respectability, Vyshinsky, said:

'History demonstrates that under Socialism . . . law is raised to the highest level of development.'[28]

The ideological foundation for this rehabilitation of law was the newly-rediscovered axiom that the ideological superstructure, though stemming from, and conditioned by, the economic base, also exerts a reflexive action upon the latter, characterised by Stalin as the 'tremendous organising, mobilising and transforming value of new ideas, new political views and new political institutions.'[29] Vyshinsky and his associates were readily able to elaborate a denunciation of bourgeois law and of the legal 'nihilists' (to whose views he had himself once partially adhered[30]); they were in a less advantageous position as regards formulating a positive theory of law. They had, essentially, to reconcile the irreconcilable; the elaboration of

[18]

objective legal norms on the one hand, and the perpetuation of discretionary powers, formulations and institutions on the other. Socialist law had to acquire some wider sanction than that of economic materialism, but without throwing overboard the dialectical framework imposed upon it by Marxism-Leninism. The watchword could no longer be 'revolutionary consciousness', nor could 'social danger' serve as the sole determinant of what was criminal and what was not.

The process of switching over to the establishment of judicial norms, of legalising the establishment, has been going on ever since 1936. So long as Stalin was alive, and particularly in the 1936-40 period, it suffered from the very great drawback of having to make allowances for the intensive use of political coercion. Thus the procedures used in the 1936-38 purge trials, the existence of the Special Board (which dealt 'as a rule [with] those cases for which sufficient evidence had not been gathered for handing the accused over to the court'[31]), the norms applicable to most 'counter-revolutionary' offences, the wholesale deportation of nationality groups, and the absence of any effective limitations on the powers of the police apparatus—all ran counter to one or more of the judicial principles proclaimed in the 1936 Constitution, in the Judiciary Act of 1938,[32] and even in the various legal codes. The primacy of politics bedevilled the achievement of legal stabilisation.

THE KHRUSHCHEV ERA AND AFTER

The process of stabilising legal institutions started in earnest after Stalin's death. On the one hand, the apparatus of coercion was gradually reduced and, on the other, the work of legal codification, which had in the preceding two decades showed few signs of getting beyond the stage of drafts despite intermittent efforts both before and after the war, accelerated. As envisaged in the 1936 Constitution, many of the All-Union Codes of the 1920s, long since obsolescent, were rewritten concurrently with the repeal of the more notoriously coercive acts of the purge era. The 1958 All-Union Bases of Criminal and Criminal Procedural Law and the derivative Republican Codes introduced a perceptible measure of liberalisation. Soviet lawyers benefited from a greater tolerance of genuine debate, even though the officially sponsored denunciation of Vyshinsky's contributions to legal theory was somewhat of a red herring.

However, while the institutional leeway was being made up, a new trend towards the substitution of communal sanctions for judicial process was being actively promoted, with the evident approval of the Party authorities. Under the new stage of the 'all people's State' (the attainment of which was proclaimed in 1961), as one Soviet jurist put it:

'The condemnation by society of anti-social actions, the moral boycotting of law-breakers, will come in ever-increasing measure to replace measures of State coercion. These latter measures will themselves change and become increasingly more akin to measures of public conditioning. Under these conditions the distinction between the law as a system of rules established by the State and applied by the organs of State power and good conduct as a code of moral demands directly created by the force of public opinion and operated solely by the force of public opinion will be increasingly smoothed away.'[33]

In line with this trend it was predicated that with the attainment of full Communism law would wither away (as foreseen by Marx and Engels) and be replaced by voluntary self-discipline based on the three elements of customary compliance, personal conviction and financial control. In the meantime, however, the struggle against crime was not to be slackened but intensified, with the emphasis on individualisation of punishment to allow for the redeemable to be redeemed and the irredeemable to be exemplarily punished.

'The transition to Communism will be accompanied by a strengthening of repressive measures not only *vis-à-vis* bribe-takers and murderers but also *vis-à-vis* all other criminals because intolerance of all crime is growing.'[34]

Although the extra-legal institutions and procedures (dealt with in Chapter V) survived Khrushchev's dismissal in 1964 largely intact, the ideological justification for them was weakened. The new leaders appeared to lack enthusiasm for the concept of the 'all people's State',[35] even if theoreticians continued to refer to it in their writings. Correspondingly, it was suggested that too much emphasis had been laid on the extra-legal institutions to the detriment of State organs.[36] A central (Union-Republican) Ministry for the Preservation of Public Order was established, with authority over similar Ministries in the Republics. Simultaneously, it was the militia

—not the comrades' courts—which was granted certain summary powers in cases of 'hooliganism'.[37] These and other developments were eloquent of a more professional trend in the fight against the worrying crime rate.

More generally, it must be remembered that however considerable the measure of stabilisation achieved, law can never be an ultimate safeguard in Soviet conditions; the notion of the 'rule of law' is not only alien to Communist thought but condemned by it;[38] no division into public and private law is recognised;[39] as a regulatory mechanism it ultimately regulates justice not in the interests of the individual or of any objective norms but primarily in those of the Soviet State and the Communist Party, claimed to be the highest embodiment of both the individual and all the component parts of society. The fact that Soviet law 'always reveals its class, political essence'[40] means that definitions of crime and the administration of justice itself continue to depend on changeable political criteria.

SOURCES

1. RSFSR *Laws*, 1917, 4:50.
2. Karev, *Organizatsiya Suda i Prokuratury*, p. 76.
3. *Encyclopaedia of State and Law*, 1925–27, p. 1593— quoted in Gsovsky, Vol. 1, p. 170.
4. RSFSR *Laws*, 1918, 44: 533.
5. RSFSR *Laws*, 1917, 4:50.
6. RSFSR *Laws*, 1919, 66: 590.
7. RSFSR *Laws*, 1918, 76–7: 818.
8. RSFSR *Laws*, 1918, 87–8: 905.
9. RSFSR *Laws*, 1922, 69: 202.
10. RSFSR *Laws*, 71:904.
11. RSFSR *Laws*, 20–1:230.
12. RSFSR *Laws*, 15:153.
13. RSFSR *Laws*, 68:901.
14. RSFSR *Laws*, 70:903.
15. RSFSR *Laws*, 1924, 86: 870.
16. RSFSR *Laws*, 1926, 82: 612.
17. RSFSR *Laws*, 80:600.
18. RSFSR *Laws*, 1922, 15:153 (Article 10 of 1922, RSFSR Criminal Code).
19. *Sorok Let Sovetskogo Prava*, p. 511; and *Sotsialisticheskaya Zakonnost*, No. 6, 1962, p. 46.
20. Stalin, *Problems of Leninism*, p. 345.
21. Pashukhanis' 1930 speech on the Soviet State and the Revolution of Law—quoted in Berman, pp. 33–4.
22. Vyshinsky, p. 24.
23. Stalin, Works, Vol. 12, p. 381.
24. *Sorok Let Sovetskogo Prava*, p. 511.

25. Stalin, *Problems of Leninism*, p. 538.
26. *Ibid.*, pp. 679–712.
27. *Ibid.*, p. 797.
28. Berman, p. 45.
29. Stalin, *Problems of Leninism*, pp. 726–7.
30. Berman, p. 45.
31. *Sovetskoye Gosudarstvo i Pravo*, No. 3, 1965, p. 27 (Zhogin).
32. Law of August 16, 1938 (*Vedomosti Verkhovnogo Soveta SSSR*, No. 11, 1938).
33. *Sovetskoye Gosudarstvo i Pravo*, No. 2, 1960, p. 27 (Article by Romashkin).
34. *Sovetskoye Gosudarstvo i Pravo*, No. 1, 1964, p. 97 (Remenson).
35. Brezhnev did not mention it at the XXIII Congress (in contrast to his endorsement at the XXII: *Pravda*, October 21, 1961). Shortly afterwards, the phrase was dropped from the bi-annual anniversary slogans (compare slogan 97, *Pravda*, April 17, 1966, with No. 99 *ibid.*, October 23, 1965.
36. *Sovetskoye Gosudarstvo i Pravo*, No. 5, 1966, p. 8 (editorial). Earlier it had been stated that the transfer of functions from State to public organisations was a complex process requiring lengthy preparation: *Politicheskoye Samoobrazovanie*, No. 12, 1964, p. 28 (Blinov).
37. *Vedomosti Verkhovnogo Soveta SSSR*, No. 30, 1966, pp. 582–6. This fact was recognised in *Sovetskoye Gosudarstvo i Pravo*, No. 2, 1967, p. 16 (Samoshchenko).
38. *Yuridichesky Slovar*, p. 494 (Article on *Pravovoe Gosudarstvo*). *Sovetskaya Yustitsiya*, No. 24, 1967, pp. 4–5 (Guliev).
39. *Sorok Let Sovetskogo Prava*, p. 605.
40. Gertsenzon, p. 6.

II

The Judiciary and the Organs of Judicial Administration

The formal structure of the Soviet judicial system has changed almost beyond recognition since 1917. The process of building institutions, however, was lengthy. The apparatus of the Prosecutor's Office did not come into existence until 1922,[1] and was not centralised on an All-Union basis until 1933:[2] a specific Soviet body of defence lawyers was created in 1922[3] but was not put on a uniform footing until 1932,[4] nor was it given final definition until 1939.[5] Though the earliest decree on the courts dates back to 1917,[6] no overall uniform act on the judiciary was put through until 1938.[7] The process of institutional change continued after the war and it cannot be assumed that it has now received final shape with the enactments of the past few years, or indeed that it will ever receive it. In 1955 the Prosecutor's Office was the subject of redefinition;[8] in 1957 the Supreme Court;[9] enactments of December, 1958,* perceptibly altered the structure, powers and terms of reference of the courts; in 1960 the RSFSR enacted its own law on Judicial

* These were the following enactments, all dated December 25, 1958, of the USSR Supreme Soviet (*Vedomosti Verkhovnogo Soveta*, No. 1, 1959):

    (*a*) Bases of Criminal Legislation of the USSR and the Union Republics.
    (*b*) Law on the Abolition of Deprivation of Electoral Rights by the Courts.
    (*c*) Law on Criminal Liability for State Crimes.
    (*d*) Law on Criminal Liability for Military Crimes.
    (*e*) Bases of Legislation on the Judicial Structure of the USSR and the Union and Autonomous Republics.
    (*f*) Law on the Alteration of the Procedure for the Election of People's Courts.
    (*g*) Regulations on Military Tribunals.
    (*h*) Bases of Criminal Judicial Procedure of the USSR and the Union Republics.

Procedure; and in 1962 a new regulatory decree on defence lawyers was adopted in the RSFSR.

It should, however, be borne in mind that the two halves of the Soviet judicial system, the judiciary proper (courts, judges, people's assessors and defence counsel), and the judicial administration, are intricately interrelated, not only with each other but also with the police system as a whole. They are all, in differing degrees, representatives of State power and the principle of the separation of the judiciary from the Executive has not been accepted in the Soviet Union. In the words of a leading Soviet jurist:

'The court is the active, effective executor of State policy, a participant in the construction of Communism.'[10]

THE JUDICIARY

(a) The Court System

The present structure of the Soviet court system is in effect triple-tiered; people's courts, regional courts, and Supreme Courts.

People's Courts exist in rural districts and towns; formerly their number in any given district was determined by population, but under the enactments of December, 1958, and subsequent derivative acts in the various constituent Republics each district (or town not divided into districts) now has only one court, the size of which varies in accordance with the density of population.[11] They function solely as courts of first instance.

Regional Courts include *oblast, krai*, town, autonomous *oblast* and national *okrug* courts; one such court in each of the types of region. They function as courts of first and second instance and have appellate jurisdiction.*

Supreme Courts are divided on a territorial basis into the Supreme Courts of the Autonomous Republics, Union Republics and, finally, of the USSR. (In addition to the above, there is also within the Armed Forces a system of military tribunals, headed by the Military Collegium of the USSR Supreme Court.)

The People's Courts have no fixed functional subdivisions. All other courts include a collegium for civil cases and a col-

* For a definition of what is meant by appellate procedure (i.e. cassation, supervisory protest, etc.) *see* pp. 59–67.

legium for criminal cases. All regional courts have a presidium; so, too, do the Supreme Courts of Autonomous Republics, and the overwhelming majority of Supreme Courts in the Union Republics have set up their own presidiums.[12] Only the Supreme Courts of the Union Republics and of the USSR form their own plenums, which meet at least once every three months. In addition, the Supreme Court includes a Military Collegium.

The various collegiums function both as courts of first instance and as courts of appeal for cases passed from lower courts; at republican and All-Union level they also function as courts of supervisory jurisdiction (i.e. for supervisory protests) with respect to lower courts. The various presidiums do not act as courts of first instance but as courts of appeal for the most part *vis-à-vis* decisions entered by the collegiums to which they are attached (e.g. the presidium of a regional court reviews protests and appeals against decisions of the criminal collegium at that same court) and also as courts of supervisory jurisdiction chiefly in relation to lower courts. The plenums of the Republic Supreme Courts issue subordinate courts with guidance on RSFSR judicial legislation, and raise points of interpretation of RSFSR legislation with the Presidium of the RSFSR Supreme Court, while the USSR Supreme Court Plenum performs similar functions at the All-Union level, in addition to reviewing on protest from the Prosecutor-General decisions of Republican Plenums which conflict with All-Union legislation.

The members of each court collegium are drawn from the members of the given court, and, in the case of the USSR Supreme Court, their composition is confirmed by the USSR Supreme Soviet. All presidiums consist of the Chairman of the court, the deputy chairmen and a fixed number of members of the court; plenums consist of the chairman, deputy chairmen and all members of the given court.

When sitting as a court of first instance (i.e. both People's Courts and collegiums of higher courts), all hearings must be conducted in the presence of one judge (the Chairman or a member of the given court) and two people's assessors; as an appellate court (i.e. any collegium) in the presence of three members of the court. For the supervisory jurisdiction exercised by the presidiums the required quorum is a simple majority.

The jurisdictional competence of the courts is graduated in

[25]

terms of the gravity of the offence. At the lowest level, the People's Courts are defined in the RSFSR Criminal Procedure Code as having jurisdiction over all cases 'other than those falling within the jurisdiction of higher courts or military tribunals'.[13] This would cover the following offences:

(a) *State Crimes*
  evasion of military service;
  illegal entry and departure into the USSR,
  certain traffic offences,
  currency speculation;
(b) (all) *Crimes Against State Property;*
(c) *Crimes Against the Life, Health, Liberty and Dignity of the Individual* (with the sole exception of aggravated murder);
(d) (all) *Crimes Against the Political and Working Rights of Citizens.*
(e) (all) *Crimes Against the Private Property of Citizens;*
(f) *Economic Crimes* (with the sole exception of the output of sub-standard production);
(g) (all) *Crimes by Officials;*
(h) *Crimes Against Justice* (with the exception of: criminal prosecution of anyone known to be innocent; the delivering of a wittingly unjust sentence; wittingly unlawful arrest; the extortion of evidence under threats; and the concealment or non-reporting of crimes);
(i) (all) *Crimes Against the Administrative Order;*
(j) (all) *Crimes Against Public Safety, Public Order and Health.*

At the next level the regional courts deal[14] with eight of the listed ten 'especially dangerous State Crimes', including, for example, treason, terrorism, sabotage, and anti-Soviet propaganda; half of the 'other State Crimes' including disclosure of State secrets, banditry and mass disorder; and with various heterogeneous crimes, including aggravated murder. The Supreme Court of each Republic, to take the RSFSR as an example, has jurisdiction over 'cases of special complexity or special public significance'.

At the highest level the USSR Supreme Court, apart from its appellate work, is entitled to hear all cases, both criminal and civil, 'of exceptional importance', and can, if it deems fit, take over any case for checking from any court throughout the country, whether or not sentence has been passed.[15]

(b) Judges

Just as the Soviet courts as a whole are termed independent, without this designation having any ultimate validity, so, too, the elaborate system by which Soviet judges are elected, and their immunity protected, cannot obscure the fact of their having to work very much within a framework determined only partly by legal considerations.

The formal provision of the 1936 Constitution, requiring the election of judges, was not honoured until December, 1948, when such elections were first held.[16] Anyone can be a judge who possesses the right to vote and is not under 25 years old. All judges now serve for a five-year term (until 1958, People's Court judges had served for only three years).[17] The judges of the Supreme Courts are elected by the corresponding Supreme Soviet; those of the regional courts by the regional Soviets; and the people's judges (in the People's Courts) by general elections in the appropriate districts as candidates of the 'Communist and non-Party bloc'. The electoral procedure for people's judges is reminiscent of that for electing members to the Supreme Soviet. Thus the candidates presented as people's judges at the 1965 elections were said to have obtained 99·56 per cent of the total number of votes cast throughout the Soviet Union.[18] The right to nominate candidates belongs to 'Communist Party organisations, trade unions, co-operatives, youth organisations, cultural societies and also general assemblies of workers and employees . . . peasants and servicemen'.[19] The 'overwhelming majority' of people's judges are said to be Communists.[20] Few figures have been given for the number of judges, either in the court system as a whole or within the People's Courts. It appears that in 1960, about 7,150 people's judges were elected,[21] 232 of them in Moscow.[22]

There are no constitutional requirements for judges to possess any minimum of legal training or experience. Though the percentage of people's judges who have had previous practical experience is high—in 1965, 76 per cent of those elected in the USSR had previously served as people's judges[23]—the overall level of legal training is still not impressive; 80·9 per cent of people's judges elected in 1965 were said to have received a higher legal education,[24] a figure expected to rise to 86 per cent in the following few years.[25] Suggestions that it should be laid down that people's judges 'must, as a rule, have higher or secondary legal training'[26] were not incorporated into the enactments of December, 1958. Debate about the educational qualification of judges continues.[27]

For their promotion and advancement judges at all stages used to depend not only upon the judiciary but also, prior to their abolition, upon the Ministries of Justice which, among other duties, determined the basis upon which awards for good work were to be made within the judicial apparatus.[28] Judges had even on occasion been drawn into the system of 'Socialist competition', a practice which was condemned in a circular issued by the Ministry of Justice of the USSR and the General Prosecutor of the USSR on February 5, 1947.[29]

Judges work in joint harness with people's assessors in all hearings at all levels of the court system (other than in appellate hearings and in the supervisory jurisdiction falling to the presidiums). A verdict can only be reached on the basis of a simple majority of the three votes involved—that of the judge and those of the two people's assessors. The judge can in theory be overruled by his colleagues: however, such cases are only reported very rarely, and then in a context which suggests that they are exceptional examples which should be followed by normally all too passive people's assessors.[30] On the other hand, there are occasional references to cases where the judge has illegally overruled both people's assessors and recorded a judgment in the face of two dissenting opinions.[31] Such practices run directly counter to Article 306 of the RSFSR Criminal Procedure Code.

Under current legislation the immunity of judges remains where it stood in 1938. Judges cannot be prosecuted at law, removed from their posts in consequence of such prosecution, or subjected to arrest, save with the consent of the Supreme Soviet of the Union Republic, or of the USSR, or of the Presidiums of either, as appropriate.[32] Equally they cannot in law be removed before expiry of their term of office save by recall from their electors, or from the organ that elected them or as a result of a court sentence.[33] To date the consequence of there having been no explicit procedure for recalling judges seems not to have conferred any practical immunity upon them but to have made their security of tenure far more dependent upon the organs of legal administration than upon their giving satisfaction to their electorate. As one prominent Soviet jurist declared:

'According to our legislation the right to remove judges and people's assessors of their duties belongs to the electors. In practice, however, the judges and people's assessors are removed only on the initiative of the State organisations. The fact is that although 18 years have passed since the ratification of the Law on the Judicial Structure of the USSR, Union and Autonomous Republics, the method of removal of judges and people's assessors has never been regulated by law.'[34]

Although the new (1960) RSFSR Law on Judicial Structure refers in passing to the removal of judges, there have since been further hints that in practice the first thing that electors know about their judge having been recalled is when they are notified of the holding of new elections.[35] In 1965, a new decree established that judges could be elected by smaller electoral districts than hitherto.[36] The writer of a subsequent book referred to the 'great difficulties' formerly involved in the premature replacement of a judge[37]:

'It was practically impossible to ensure that the voters had the right of recalling people's judges in large towns and districts ... because in order to vote on the recall it was necessary to get together all the voters living in the given town or district. ... Therefore sometimes the necessary recall ... was put off; the people's judge who had compromised himself was released from work at his own request or for some such reason. This had a negative effect on the education of judicial cadres and created an atmosphere of impunity'.[38]

(c) People's Assessors

The people's assessors date back as an institution to 1917.[39] Their present resemblance to a jury begins and ends with the fact that they are not part of the judicial establishment; that they serve only for a period of two weeks in the year over a period of five years; and that they are not paid a salary. They are more akin to non-professional co-judges. In fact, their numerical resemblance to a jury panel has declined over the years. In March, 1918, hearings of criminal cases were conducted in the presence of 12 people's assessors:[40] in November, 1918, this number was reduced to six for certain criminal cases and to two for others.[41] This latter disposition remained in force until 1922, when the new RSFSR Court Regulations,[42] after heated arguments,[43] fixed the maximum number of people's assessors participating in court hearings at both district and regional level at two, where it remains today. According to P. Stuchka, a leading political and legal figure of the early Soviet period, this reduction was dictated by economic considerations; it had been intended to revert to a larger number subsequently.[44]

At present, panels of people's assessors are attached to all courts, up to and including the USSR Supreme Court. The total number empanelled for the People's Courts alone in 1965 was more than 517,000.[45] Some 44 per cent of people's assessors have been said to be Party members or candidate members.[46] As with judges, the only requirement of a people's assessor is that he be 25 years of age or over, and in possession of electoral rights. The electoral procedure for people's assessors repeats that for judges, with the difference, introduced in December, 1958, that those empanelled for the People's Courts are now elected at general meetings of factory workers, collective farmers, etc., at their place of work or residence;[47] those for all other courts are elected by the corresponding local Soviets and Supreme Soviets who elect (though 'elect' scarcely does justice to the situation where lists of up to a thousand names are presented for consideration) the judges of the various higher courts up to and including the USSR Supreme Court. People's assessors elected to People's Courts perform their service within a two-year period; those elected to higher courts, within a five-year period. Despite the people's assessors' formal responsibility for assisting in arriving at a verdict, they normally have little or no legal training. Eighty per cent of the people's assessors questioned in a survey in a regional town of the RSFSR stated that their system of legal training should be changed. Some 60 per cent took no regular part in the courses arranged for them.[48]

The people's assessors normally attend court for not more than two weeks in the year, during which period they retain their wages at their normal place of work,[49] or if they are not workers or employees, other financial arrangements are made (hitherto existing regulations provided for the payment in such cases of a daily allowance of 10 roubles[50]). In the event of the temporary absence of a People's Court judge (by reason of sickness or leave) his duties are assigned by the district Soviet to one of the people's assessors.[51] The procedure for the recall of people's assessors is the same as that for judges.

As has already been noted, the views of the people's assessors are not always respected by the judges in arriving at a verdict. Soviet sources point out that even when people's assessors have qualms about a case, they find legal argument difficult and therefore tend to let the judge have his way.[52] As one writer put it:

'Unfortunately, it is not rare for the equal rights of the assessors and the judge ... to be reduced to the active rôle played by the presiding judge alone, and this gives rise to the opinion among citizens that the "judge passed sentence".'[53]

Elsewhere it has been regretted that people's assessors 'extremely rarely' bother to take notes during a trial.[54] Though the procedural legislation of December, 1958, has left the position of people's assessors largely where it stood in 1938, there had been some advocacy of strengthening the system of people's assessors. It had, for instance, been suggested that the established practice of people's assessors attending the pre-trial preparatory session of the court, which decides whether or not to confirm the findings of the preliminary investigation and to hold a trial, should be extended to allow them to participate in the preparatory sessions of all other court hearings (i.e. second instance ones). At present they are excluded.[55] This did not meet with approval and instances where the extension was practised had already been denounced by the USSR Supreme Court Plenum in rulings for 1950, 1953 and 1957.[56] A more significant suggestion, which has not been put into practice, was that in certain criminal cases the number of people's assessors participating in the hearing should be increased to six, which would enable the question of guilt and innocence and of the degree of guilt of the accused to be 'decided more correctly by a wider collegium than one consisting of three persons'.[57] A corollary to this, which earned condemnation as being at variance with Lenin's teaching,[58] was that[59]

'the decision of the question of the guilt of the accused in some categories of crimes should be transferred to the competence of the people's assessors. In form this would resemble trial by jury ... Such a division of duties between the judge and the people's assessors would heighten the rôle, activity and responsibility of the latter ... At the same time this would not in the least detract from the rôle of the judges for they would continue to be fully responsible for the conduct of the trial.'

Despite the fact that both reforms were rejected in the drafting of the All-Union legislation of 1958 and subsequent Republican legislation, including the 1961 RSFSR Criminal Code, it is noteworthy that the main proponents of such changes still continued to canvass the minority view.[60] Additionally they suggested that *raion* People's Courts should have the right to sit with one judge and either two or six people's assessors, which would increase the 'self-reliance and independence' of the latter *vis-à-vis* the former,[61] or that the number of assessors in certain kinds of cases (e.g. capital ones) should at least be increased.[62]

(d) Defence Lawyers

Though defence counsel have been provided for in one form or another since 1918, the so-called 'collegiums of legal defenders'[63] remained in existence only for seven months up to October, 1918,[64] owing to what was described as the 'impossibility of including in their ranks defenders from the experienced specialists of the bourgeois defence counsel who then stood to a man on the side of the enemies of the working class'.[65] From 1922 until about 1928, virtually all legal defence was on the basis of individual practice.[66] The process of rounding up all defence lawyers into 'collegiums of advocates' was not put through until the period 1928–30; it was characterised by

'instances of the compulsory "collectivisation of defence", of illegal utilisation of the funds of the collectives for the needs of court and prosecuting organs, and of the deprivation of advocates who had not joined a collective of any real possibility of appearing in court'.[67]

These new collegiums were given legal shape by a regulation of February 27, 1932.[68] The All-Union regulations of August, 1939, defining the organisation of Soviet defence lawyers have now been replaced by republican legislation:[69] the currently valid regulatory order for all RSFSR defence lawyers dates from July, 1962.[70] No over-all figure is available for the total number of Soviet defence lawyers but in 1964 there were in the RSFSR 73 collegiums comprising more than 7,000 members.[71] There are about 1,000 in Moscow.[72]

All defence lawyers are organised into collegiums. These collegiums exist in all *oblasts, krais* and Autonomous Republics and in Moscow and Leningrad. It has been a cause for complaint[73] that in some Union Republics the collegiums are subordinated to the local Councils of Ministers, in others to the Judicial Commissions attached to the latter, whereas in yet others (e.g. the RSFSR, the Ukraine and Kazakhstan[74]) control over them is exercised by the local Soviets' Executive Committees. Such organisational disparity was said to lead sometimes to unsuccessful direction.[75] Each collegium sets up 'consulting points' in the districts and towns under the area served by it. The day-to-day work of the members of each collegium is performed within whichever 'consulting point' they are attached to. The tasks of the defence lawyers cover[76]

(a) the giving of legal advice;
(b) the drawing up of statements, defence protests and other documents for individuals or organisations;
(c) participation as defence counsel in criminal and civil cases.

They also provide State enterprises with legal consultation and other services on a contractual basis. The status of such consultants within enterprises is often low.[77]

Members of collegiums must have higher legal education and either have done two years' work as a jurist or undergo six months' training; or, exceptionally, if without higher legal education they may be admitted on the strength of not less than five years' work as a jurist.[78] In practice, however, the number of such exceptions is high: in the RSFSR, 20 per cent of lawyers were said in 1965 to lack a higher education. (Included in this figure were some who only had a primary or incompleted secondary education and whose legal knowledge derived from courses. Despite their unsatisfactory work, they were not expelled from their collegiums.[79]) Any criminal record or 'moral or professional' unsuitability involves disbarment for prospective members or, for existing members in extreme cases, expulsion.[80] Complaints about unethical practices by lawyers themselves are nevertheless not rare.[81]

A general meeting of all the members of a collegium elects its presidium, which controls the enrolment of new members and the apportionment of fees received as salaries. It also has the right to apply disciplinary measures to members, including reprimands, and expulsion (in extreme cases). A leading lawyer has made this revealing remark while complaining about the lack of a single disciplinary system:

'Up to now, certain collegiums still do not have a clear idea of what constitutes a disciplinary offence. Sometimes it is considered that if a lawyer pleads for acquittal but the court convicts, the lawyer is liable to answer for a breach of discipline'.[82]

Protests against non-admission or expulsion can be submitted to the appropriate regional or town Soviet Executive Committee within a month.

There had been the odd plea from the defence lawyers themselves that they should be 'autonomous' and exercise supervision over themselves, which in a sense would be in keeping with the emphasis laid on their being a voluntary organisation. However, despite a measure of debate[83] on this subject the 1962 RSFSR law provided for an intermediate solution (i.e. between the extremes of autonomy and unadulterated Ministerial supervision).

Overall scales of payment have been hitherto laid down in the form of instructions, the text of which has not normally been published in the past. It appears that up to its abolition in April, 1963, the RSFSR Ministry of Justice had been leaning on the system devised by the old USSR Ministry of Justice in 1955 subject to certain modifications,[84] and also to the divergent practices of the collegiums themselves. After 1955, most RSFSR collegiums worked to a system advocated by its Ministry of Justice which guaranteed a minimum wage, above which the scale rose in relation to the amount of work done by each member.[85] However, a rival system which apparently gained ground provided for no increase in salary where work was fulfilled by over 200 per cent and only a slight one where this was over 150 per cent, together with a salary reduction for under-fulfilment.[86] Against this background there was also a dispute over whether or not defence lawyers should be paid fixed salaries. Some urged that this would reduce the cash incentive inducing the defence to 'win their case' irrespective of truth.[87] This view did not meet with agreement among defence lawyers[88] who evidently detected behind it the far-reaching argument that professional (i.e. paid) defence counsel was a superfluous luxury.[89] In 1965, after further discussion of the merits of various systems of payment,[90] a model Regulatory Order on lawyers' earnings and a model tariff for legal assistance were published to provide a basis for action in the Union Republics.[91] (Two years later, however, it was still being suggested that lawyers should receive a regulated salary and not be paid by results.[92] This suggests that there has been no hurry to implement the model Regulatory Order.)

The regulations laid down a monthly payment norm which ranged from 160 roubles in Moscow and Leningrad and the surrounding regions down to 140 in the lowest category of towns and districts; probationers were to receive 75 roubles. These figures were to be used in calculating the actual monthly salary as follows: the lawyer was allowed to retain at least 70 per cent of the money paid for his services (up to the limit of the norm applicable in his case). A percentage, to be decided on by a general meeting of his collegium, was to be deducted for its reserve fund (the 'collegium presidium's fund'). Should there be any earnings left over and above the lawyer's norm, he was entitled to received from 50 to 70 per cent of them (this depended on the type of client) provided that this additional sum did not exceed half his stipulated norm. Should his earnings drop below 75 roubles a month, the presidium of his collegium would, in valid cases, make them up to this minimum figure.

A potential bone of contention in the new regulations was the method of allocating work to lawyers. Previous regulations had stated that this was done by the head of the legal consultation section in accordance with the qualifications of the lawyers 'and personal requests to him'[93] (i.e. a particular lawyer could be chosen by members of the public or defendants, a right commonly exercised[94]). The phrase concerning 'personal requests' was lacking from the text of the model regulations published in 1965. There is a suggestion that in certain "especially important cases" (i.e. with political overtones) defence lawyers may need a special permit before participating.[95]

Also laid down in 1965 was an established scale of charges ranging from the two roubles payable for drawing up certain legal documents to a maximum of 250 roubles for participation 'in a particularly complex case in exceptional instances' which involved several defendants or which lasted over a week. (Should a case continue for over 10 days, an additional 10 roubles for each extra day was payable, irrespective of the number of people defended by the lawyer.) However, the maximum payment for a routine one-day criminal case in a court of first instance was only 25 roubles. (In certain cases no payment needs to be made by the client or he is released from his obligation to pay.[96])

Defence counsel are thus not among the best-paid section of

the Soviet intelligentsia. Perhaps for that reason earnings 'on the side' from clients are not a rare phenomenon.[97]

Apart from court hearings, in which the work of the defence lawyers is predominantly concerned with criminal cases, the main bulk of legal consultation and legal aid work appears to be concerned with housing problems, family law, or criminal proceedings. A breakdown of the number of consultations, etc., given by a Moscow *raion* 'consulting point' several years ago was:[98]

Housing	2,234
Family law	1,760
Criminal Cases	1,630
Civil law	860
Pensions	844
Labour matters	642
Redress of injury	550
Inheritance law	264

Under the All-Union dispensations of December, 1958, as well as under the subsequent RSFSR Code of Criminal Procedure, the defence lawyer is

(a) allowed access to his client when the preliminary investigation is completed, save in the case of those under 18 or physically or mentally incapacitated where he may be admitted to the case at the stage of preferment of charges by the investigator; and

(b) not admitted to participate in the pre-trial or trial stages of cases for which only 'inquiry' by the militia (as distinct from a 'preliminary investigation') constitutes the pre-trial procedure.

Both these provisions have been the subject of active and continued debate, affecting as they do the stage and scale at which the legal defence operates. The present provisions mark an advance on the previous dispensation whereby defence lawyers were not admitted until the case actually came up for trial, but do not go as far as some Soviet lawyers had suggested from the mid-1930s onwards and are still suggesting[99]—that he be admitted towards the beginning of the preliminary investigation when charges are preferred—a state of affairs which was actually in force 'in the early days of Soviet rule'.[100] An empowering amendment to this effect advocated by senior Soviet

[36]

lawyers was rejected in 1958 on the grounds that it would 'prolong the period of the preliminary investigation and perceptibly fetter the operational scope of the investigator in collecting data'.[101] Earlier on it had supposedly been opposed by *inter alia* the 'majority of executive committees' in the RSFSR,[102] a possible hint that if the proponents were lawyers the opponents were policemen. More or less the same fate awaited the proposal for admitting defence lawyers to pre-trial 'inquiry' which was not adopted,[103] though this did not silence its advocates.[104] There have been influential hints that it might still be adopted.[105]

At the court hearing, the attendance of a defence lawyer is mandatory in cases where a State prosecutor is present. In certain circumstances the accused may conduct his own defence. The findings of the court of first instance can be protested by the accused, or, as is mostly the case, by the defence lawyer on his behalf to a higher instance.[106] The 1961 regulations provide only for optional participation of defence counsel in the court of second instance, though the desirability of this being made obligatory had been urged by some lawyers.[107]

In fact, this is a step backward from Article 409 of the earlier RSFSR Criminal Code[108] which had made the presence of the parties involved obligatory, and which had been interpreted to cover the presence of the defence lawyer, even though this had been frequently violated in practice.[109] On the other hand, in belated accordance with the tenor of Article 111 of the USSR Constitution, Article 8 of the 1938 Judiciary Act providing for open trials in all cases, and with lawyers' suggestions,[110] provision has now been made to allow defence counsel to be summoned to the hearing of supervisory protests, at least in the RSFSR.[111]

The notional position of the Soviet defence lawyer is, however, an important factor in shaping his attitude to his client. What is termed the 'bourgeois' or 'apolitical'[112] conception of the lawyer's relation to his client is totally rejected:

'The Soviet defence lawyer cannot convert himself into the servant of his client, blindly following him in the defence of his interests, even though those interests are not legal and detract from, rather than contribute to, the interests of Socialist justice. In defending the rights and legal interests of his client, the Soviet defence lawyer must stop short at the brink where truth ends and falsehood begins, where the interests of the State and society are

[37]

damaged by the counterposing to them of the illegal interests of his client. The "eternal" problem of bourgeois defence counsel concerning the right of the defence to lie [sic] was discarded from the very first in Soviet criminal procedure.'[113]

There are nevertheless other divergences on the subject evident among Soviet lawyers. There has been a sharp conflict between those who see in the defence lawyers 'the court's assistant'[114] there primarily to help ascertain the facts, incriminating or extenuating, and those who regard him as 'the representative of the accused'.[115] The latter, it is suggested, stress the rôle of the defence lawyer's 'inner conviction', would not require him to ascertain for himself the guilt or innocence of his client but urge him to step out boldly in defence of his client.[116] This dichotomy in part accounts for the Janus-like nature of some of the pronouncements on what Soviet defence counsel is to do in a given situation. There is a tendency towards such pronouncements as:

'he must not defend at all costs ... Defence of the criminal must not transform itself into defence of the crime'[117]

or

'divergences in court between the lawyer and his client on the question of the proven-ness or unproven-ness of the accusation are an extremely undesirable phenomenon'[118]

or that he must protect

'not only the personal interests of the accused but also the interests of society and, therefore, of the State'.[119]

Generally speaking, however, the more generous view of the lawyers' duties seems to be prevailing and one authority has gone on record that the lawyer can plead for an acquittal even when he is himself convinced merely that inadequate proof has been established to demonstrate his client's guilt.[120]

The official Soviet view is that:

'The Soviet defence lawyer is bound to be a propagandist of the Marxist-Leninist world-outlook and of Communist morals in all his activity. In pronouncing his speech of defence, the lawyer must devote attention to the education of both his client and those present at the trial in the spirit of Communist ideology, adding his modest contribution to the cause of eradicating crime and educating the new man.'[121]

Within this framework the Soviet defence lawyer must bring to the court's attention all that is in favour of his client and contest the accusation where it is unjustified. He cannot enter a plea of guilty where his client does not acknowledge his guilt.[122] It would not be unfair to say that the path to be steered is not an easy one. It has been pointed out that defence lawyers often lean over backwards; they 'have laid down their arms prematurely and stopped fighting, sometimes causing the condemnation of innocent people'; they frequently 'assume the attitude in court of the public prosecutor and virtually become second accusers'; they 'behave passively in the examination of evidence, the cross-examining of defence witnesses, considering their main task to be to pronounce a "brilliant speech" '.[123] The Minister of Justice of the RSFSR himself drew attention to the fact that some defence counsel 'fear to engage in a real argument, based on principles, with representatives of the State Prosecution'.[124] In their tasks, they are not, it should be noted, always assisted by the other arms of the judiciary. The USSR Prosecutor-General had in June, 1960, to issue a circular letter to all prosecutors to remind them *inter alia* of the 'inadmissibility of hindering a defence lawyer from having an interview alone with his client' whether before or after studying the latter's case.[125] There have also been occasions when the Soviet Press has portrayed the work of Soviet defence lawyers in such a way as to give the impression 'that they are something alien to our Soviet judicial system'.[126] For that matter the pre-trial services of defence counsel are far from invariably employed: in 1964 the percentage was as low as 8–10 in all cases completed by the investigators (not including those where defence counsel's presence was obligatory).[127] This is acknowledged to be sometimes the result of investigators regarding the admission of defence counsel at this stage as a 'hindrance'.[128]

There is certainly latent discord between defence lawyers—the Cinderellas of the legal profession—on the one hand and the judiciary on the other. As the head of the Moscow *oblast* collegium of defence lawyers revealed in retaliation:

'There is a far worse thing. There exists the practice under which jurists (judges, investigators, etc.) who have in some way compromised themselves are sent to work as defence lawyers. These people bring with them disrespect for the work of the jurist.'[129]

(a) The Prosecutor's Office

The Prosecutor's Office was first set up in 1922.[130] Before then the functions of prosecution had been shared somewhat haphazardly between the Soviets and the judicial organs.[131] After 1922 the powers and scope of the Prosecutor's Office rapidly increased: in 1923 it acquired powers of constitutional supervision;[132] in 1924 it acquired jurisdiction over civil cases;[133] in 1926 it was given disciplinary powers over the organs of administration;[134] in 1933 it was put on an All-Union basis.[135] For the next 22 years there was no overall regulating act on it, though the need for one became increasingly apparent, especially after the enactment of the 1936 USSR Constitution. Finally, its powers and functions were defined in a law of May 24, 1955,[136] and its structure was given formal shape in a further law of April 7, 1956.[137]

The Prosecutor's Office is headed by the USSR Prosecutor-General, who is appointed for a term of seven years by the USSR Supreme Soviet. The Prosecutor-General is responsible for the direction and appointment of the entire apparatus of the Prosecutor's Office, which is constructed, unlike the court system, on the basis of direct and uniform subordination; thus the Union Republics do not have their own General Prosecutors. A Chief Military Prosecutor's Office exists as part of the central apparatus of the Office of the USSR Prosecutor-General.[138] Subordinate prosecutors exist at Union Republic level and at all lower levels down to *oblast* and district, and the prosecutors at all these levels are appointed for five years. The entire investigatory apparatus (with the exception of that part dealing with certain State crimes, which comes under the Committee of State Security, and of the investigators subordinated to the Ministry for the Preservation of Public Order, numbers of whom have been increasing[139] since they were permitted to examine cases in 1963) forms an integral part of the Prosecutor's Office and is represented in it at all levels.* All prosecutors and investigators must have higher legal education, save in exceptional cases, and must have done one year's probationary

---

* A suggestion has even been published that the Prosecutor-General's instructions on all questions concerning preliminary investigation should be binding on the Committee of State Security and the Ministry for the Preservation of Public Order.[140]

work at district level before appointment,[141] again except in certain cases.[142] For regional and district prosecutors, the age of entry is 25 or over.[143]

The overriding duty of the Prosecutor's Office is supervision over legality, both administrative and judicial. Quite apart from the relationship of the prosecutors to the courts and to the organs of investigation (which is dealt with in detail later), they are also responsible for supervising the actions of all administrative bodies and officials from the constitutional (though this is formally denied[144]), legal and administrative points of view, and for supervising the work of prisons and corrective labour establishments.

The administrative supervision exercised by the Prosecutor's Office over all Ministries, factories, local Soviets, etc., is said to be distinct from the functional control exercised by such bodies as the Soviets themselves, the organs of State control, and the individual Ministries, over their subordinate departments in that : (a) it represents 'supreme' supervision deriving from its empowerment by the Supreme Soviet; (b) it is directed towards securing uniform observance of laws throughout the USSR; and (c) it carries with it no power of immediate executive control but only that of protest, combined where appropriate with the institution of criminal proceedings.[145] For all that, it represents a very wide field of action, though a recent source has pointed out that the Prosecutor's Office has fewer rights now than previously.[146]

Prosecutors can and must check the conformity of all the orders of Ministries and Soviets to existing legislation; they can and must check complaints and other 'signals' received from the public of infringements of law by outside bodies or individuals. They must periodically check on the work of all organisations within the area they cover, even where there is no evidence of infringement. They can call in outside experts to verify instances of the 'dislocation of constructional plans, the manufacture of sub-standard goods, the poor sowing of crops, the dislocation of tractor repairs, the infringement of budgetary and financial discipline', and draw the attention of the appropriate bodies to such infringements.[147] The dividing line between legal supervision and quasi-executive control is readily overstepped. The USSR Prosecutor-General stated in 1956:

'Unjustified expansion of the general supervisory functions of the Prosecutor's Office, connected in most cases with amateurish excursions by the prosecutors into some specialised sphere or another, merely distracts the organs of the Prosecutor's Office from their real work of carrying out supervision over the exact observance of the law.'[148]

At the same time the Prosecutor's Office does not, it is said,[149] have any powers of constitutional supervision. This is the task of the Presidium of the Supreme Soviet of the USSR, which is, as it were, its own legal custodian, though the instances quoted when it has amended its unconstitutional acts are few and far between.[150] For its part, the Prosecutor's Office can make 'representations' only, not 'protests', in respect of the legislative acts of the Supreme Soviets of the Republics, and, as it would seem, it cannot do even this in respect of the USSR Supreme Soviet.[151] The Prosecutor's Office has no powers of supervising the legality of actions of the Party Central Committee or any other Party organs. On the other hand, the Party's Central Committee 'periodically discusses the USSR Prosecutor-General's reports on the state of, and measures for strengthening, legality and law and order in the country'.[152] A recent textbook has firmly defined the respective positions of the Party and the Prosecutor's Office:

'The principle of the independence of supervision by the procuracy does not, however, contradict in any degree the fulfilment of the Communist Party's leading rôle in our country'.[153]

The textbook revealed that local Party organisations give their opinion of prosecutors and investigators of the Prosecutor's Office when their testimonial certificates are made out (at least once every two years in theory).[154]

In their judicial functions, the prosecutors face in several directions at once. They direct the investigation of cases and yet control observance of the law by the investigators; they present the case for the prosecution at the trial and yet are called upon to see that the court and all the parties to the case (and, presumably, they themselves as the prosecution) observe all the procedural requirements. Neither of these antitheses has escaped the attention of Soviet lawyers, but the former has evoked the widest measure of debate. One of the counter-suggestions was that the investigatory apparatus for all criminal cases should be transferred from the Prosecutor's Office to some outside body, such as the Ministry of Justice.[155] This would, in effect, be a step nearer to the pre-1922 position, when investigation was concentrated in the hands of the court organs.[156] Indeed, the debate on this question has been going on ever since the 1920s[157] when other variants were also debated, one of which—that of creating a unified investigatory apparatus subordinate neither to the Prosecutor's Office nor to the militia or security organs—is still being resurrected.[158] Yet another suggestion which would hardly have contributed to the creation of greater safeguards, though it might have accelerated the conduct of the investigation, was that all investigations should be handed over to the militia and the prosecutors merely retain the duty of supervision over legality.[159] An even more recent contribution has been the idea that the investigative apparatus should be made into a separate organ entirely or at least partly removed from the administrative as distinct from the supervisory control of the Prosecutor's Office.[160]

It is indeed hard to see how the prosecutor can adequately discharge his two antithetical functions at once. A certain unease on this score is mirrored in the debate among Soviet lawyers between those who assign to the prosecutors as well as the investigator (within limits) a solely accusatory function in pre-trial procedure, and those who insist on the duties of both *qua* impartial investigation. Yet the prosecutor is in a sense both judge and jury. On the side of directing the investigation, he not only gives general operational guidance to the investigator,[161] but also takes part in the conduct of interrogations[162] and is, in fact, empowered himself to assume conduct of the investigation at any stage or in its totality.[163] 'He can begin, continue and complete the investigation.'[164] Doubt has been expressed, however, as to whether such intervention is compatible with his continued responsibility for safeguarding legality[165] and the suggestion voiced that this latter function be entrusted in such cases to the next senior prosecutor.[166] Yet, pursuing this trend to its logical extreme, the fact of one and the same prosecutor having taken part in the investigation of a case and subsequently conducted the prosecution in court cannot, it has been stated, form any ground for the accused to demand his replacement in court.[167] These considerations acquire meaning in the light of continued warnings against the danger of imparting an incriminating slant to the preliminary investigation.[168] Although the cases where 'those guilty of serious crimes remain undetected and escape liability while persons who have committed no crime are brought to trial' are said to be rare,[169] reports of miscarriages of justice which involve even extreme penalties[170] reflect no credit on the prosecutors initially concerned with the cases, or, by extension, on the much-vaunted system of checks they represent.

On the side of controlling the legality of the investigator's actions, it is the prosecutor who has to sanction the detention of suspects,[171] the searching of premises[172] and the confiscation of correspondence,[173] but it is the investigator, and he alone, who has to draw up the final act of accusation on the basis of which the case is taken to court.[174] It had been suggested that the prosecutor should take over this last-named function.[175] There is also the curious anomaly that the suspect or the accused, before the court hearing, can only protest against the investigator's actions to the latter's superior—i.e. the prosecutor;[176] and can only protest against the investigating prosecutor's actions not to the court but to his superior prosecutor.[177] By and large, the formulae adopted in the Bases of Criminal Judicial Procedure of December, 1958, as well as those incorporated in the derivative Codes of Criminal Procedure, though defining more clearly the rights of the investigator, do nothing to solve the question of the prosecutor's bifocal position, which has evoked such comments as:

'The prosecutor who has directed the investigation has tied himself so closely to all its merits and defects that he can hardly pretend to the necessary objectivity and boldness in his own deductions, including, for instance, public withdrawal of the charge made in the event of it being unproven.'[178]

The second antithesis of the prosecutor at the court hearing being both a party to the action and the trustee of legality for all the parties involved is equally more than academic:

'Unfortunately the fact cannot be ignored that in a number of instances prosecutors attending the court hearing concentrate their attention on their prosecuting function and do not pay sufficient attention to supervising the legality of the court's examination, do not react during the course of the hearing to the infringement of legally established rules for the conduct of the hearing.'[179]

It is hardly surprising, therefore, that "many people ... view the prosecutor as an official whose basic task consists of prosecuting criminals".[180]

Moreover, while Soviet legal authorities are in no doubt as to the prosecutor's competence and duties as counsel for the prosecution, there has been, and still is, a considerable measure of disagreement as regards his powers of supervision *vis-à-vis* the court. One school maintains that the prosecutor can have no function other than to prosecute;[181] that he has no power to suspend or countermand the court's actions other than that of his special opinion being recorded and of subsequent appellate protest; and that the court must be its own master.[182] The other school describes this as a 'liberal bourgeois interpretation',[183] emphasises that the prosecutor continues to play a dual rôle inside the court just as he does outside,[184] and argues that if, for example, the evidence for acquittal is convincing the prosecutor may find himself pronouncing a speech for the defence.[185] This question of whether or not the prosecutor should supervise the court was not cleared up in the legislation of December, 1958, nor did the RSFSR Criminal Procedural Code of 1960 give any lead on it.

The prosecutors are, at least, less procedurally limited than the courts in that there are few restrictions to prevent one and the same prosecutor dealing with the same case in its various stages, such as are very definitely imposed in the composition of the court in the successive stages of trial, re-trial and appellate jurisdiction. Not only does one and the same prosecutor normally conduct the investigation and attend the preliminary court sessions and the hearing in the court of first instance,[186] but he is also fully entitled to conduct the same case at its second hearing and even in the stage of supervisory appeal, provided that this is not ruled out by the procedural provisions which attach certain prosecutors to certain courts.[187] While the presence of a prosecutor at a criminal trial is not mandatory, and is governed by specific regulations (e.g. where complex evidence is to be presented, where the offence is punishable by deprivation of freedom, in cases of 'public significance', or where a higher prosecutor or the court so rules)[188] there has been a sharp rise in the number of criminal cases heard by courts of first instance with the participation of prosecutors. Some past figures are :1936, 9·4 per cent; 1938, 12·6 per cent; 1939, 39·9 per cent; 1940, 39·9 per cent; 1941, 35·6 per cent; 1942, 26·2 per cent; 1943, 39·5 per cent; 1944, 32·8 per cent; 1945, 40·9 per cent.[189]

In subsequent stages the presence of a prosecutor at cassation appeals has been made mandatory in the RSFSR,[190] and remains so in the case of supervisory appeals;[191] in neither case

[45]

is the presence of the accused or his defence lawyer provided for, save on a permissive basis.

(b) ex-Ministries of Justice

Up to June, 1956, overall administrative control of the judicial organs (though not of Prosecutor's Office) lay with the USSR Ministry of Justice,[192] first set up on July 20, 1936. In June, 1956, the USSR Ministry was abolished and its functions were allocated to the already existing Ministries of Justice in the Union Republics.[193] In August, 1956,[194] the regional administrations of the latter were abolished and the functions of control and scrutiny they had exercised over the local People's Courts handed over to the corresponding regional courts. Finally, between 1958 and 1963 all the Union Republican Ministries of Justice were themselves abolished and their control functions *vis-à-vis* the courts transferred to the Presidiums of the various Supreme Courts in these Republics.[195]

Before this abolition, the Republican Ministries of Justice had taken over responsibility for:

(a) the issuing of instructions and orders concerning the judicial organs;

(b) the initiating of disciplinary proceedings against judges and the 'right of final decision on the question of expulsion from a collegium of defence lawyers';[196]

(c) the organisation of the election of judges;

(d) the compilation of establishment schedules and general supervision over all judicial cadres;

(e) the regulation and organisation of training courses.

The present position is less unified and less clear-cut. The organisational consequences of the abolition of the Ministries of Justice have varied from republic to republic. In some cases (e.g. the RSFSR and Georgia) the Council of Ministers has been explicitly assigned the task of supervising and controlling the work of 'defence lawyers', in others (e.g. Armenia and Estonia) this is performed by the Juridical Commission attached to the Council of Ministers.[197] Some, though not all, republics have set up a Judicial Commission under their Council of Ministers to be responsible for, *inter alia*, the codification and systematisation of laws. On an All-Union scale the function is discharged by the Judicial Commission attached to the USSR Council of Ministers set up in May, 1956.[198] To assist it in its task, this Commission has attached to it an All-Union Scientific Research Institute of Soviet Legislation.[199] The highest common factor throughout the republics appears to be that the various Supreme Courts are to exercise scrutiny and control of the work of their own regional and district courts and to assume responsibility for the compilation of judicial statistics. Likewise, the USSR Supreme Court has certain powers of scrutiny and supervision over its republican counterparts.[200]

The abolition of Ministerial supervision received a mixed welcome from the judiciary (there had been objections to overloading the Supreme Court of the RSFSR with organisational questions).[201] Nevertheless, as time went by, there was increasing demand from jurists themselves for a return to a centralised Ministry of Justice—several stated that its abolition had been quite 'unjustified'—although not on its 'former basis', which presumably involved excessive interference with the work of the judiciary.[202] As one of the critics pointed out, the abolition had been intended to cut down the administrative apparatus and expense, but it had in fact done neither. The function of administration had been added to the proper judicial function of the Supreme (and regional) Courts, to the detriment of both. He made it clear that interference with the 'independence' of the judiciary was continuing: organs which should have confined themselves to administration were issuing edicts, etc., on court practice.[203]

SOURCES

1. RSFSR *Laws*, 1922, 36: 424.
2. USSR *Laws*, 1933, 40: 239.
3. RSFSR *Laws*, 1922, 36: 425.
4. Regulations on Defence Lawyers, adopted on February 27, 1932—Neishtadt, p. 8.
5. *Vedomosti Verkhovnogo Soveta SSSR*, No. 11, 1938.
6. RSFSR *Laws*, 1917, 4:50.
7. *Vedomosti Verkhovnogo Soveta SSSR*, No. 11, 1938.
8. *Ibid.*, No. 9, 1955.
9. *Ibid.*, No. 4, 1957.
10. *Pravovye Garantii*, p. 174.
11. *Sovetskaya Yustitsiya*, 1959, No. 2, pp. 8–9.
12. Belorussia is the odd man out: Malyarov, p. 198n.
13. 1961, RSFSR Criminal Procedure Code, art. 35.
14. *Ibid.*, art. 36.
15. Gorshenin, p. 43.
16. Perlov, *Organizatsiya Raboty Narodnogo Suda*, p. 14.
17. *Vedomosti Verkhovnogo Soveta SSSR*, No. 1, 1959:

Law on the Alteration of the Procedure for the Election of People's Courts.

18. *Byulleten Verkhovnogo Suda SSSR*, No. 1, 1966, p. 3.
19. *Vedomosti Verkhovnogo Soveta RSFSR*, No. 41, 1960 (art. 28 of Regulatory Order on Election to District People's Courts of October 28, 1960).
20. *Sovetskaya Yustitsiya*, No. 11, 1966, p. 1.
21. Sladkov, p. 7.
22. *Novoye Ugolovnoye Zakonodatelstvo RSFSR*, p. 28.
23. *Byulleten Verkhovnogo Suda SSSR*, No. 1, 1966, p. 5.
24. *Ibid.*, p. 5.
25. *Sovetskaya Yustitsiya*, No. 11, 1966, p. 1.
26. *Izvestiya*, May 18, 1958.
27. *Sotsialisticheskaya Zakonnost*, No. 9, 1966, p. 19.
28. Perlov, *Organizatsiya Raboty Sovetskogo Suda*, pp. 18–19.
29. *Ibid.*, p. 18.
30. *Sovetskaya Yustitsiya*, No. 2, 1965, p. 2; *ibid.*, No. 6, 1965, p. 1; Feifer, pp. 82–83.
31. *Sbornik Deistvuyushchikh Postanovlenii Plenuma Verkhovnogo Suda SSSR*, p. 98 (Decisions of December 1, 1950, December 4, 1953, and April 10, 1957); *Kommunist*, No. 7, 1956, p. 46 (Rakhunov), and *Sovetskoye Gosudarstvo i Pravo*, No. 4, 1962, p. 96 (Perlov); *Sovetskaya Yustitsiya*, No. 2, 1965, p. 2; *ibid.*, No. 6, 1965, p. 2.

32. December, 1958, Bases of Judicial Structure, art. 36.
33. *Ibid.*, art. 35.
34. *Kommunist*, No. 7, 1956, p. 45 (Rakhunov).
35. *Novoye Ugolovnoye Zakonodatelstvo RSFSR*, p. 22.
36. *Vedomosti Verkhovnogo Soveta SSSR*, No. 36, 1965, p. 839.
37. Sladkov, p. 3.
38. *Ibid.*, p. 4.
39. RSFSR *Laws*, 1917, 4:50.
40. RSFSR *Laws*, 1918, 26: 420.
41. *Ibid.*, 85, 889.
42. RSFSR *Laws*, 1922, 69: 902.
43. *Vestnik Moskovskogo Universiteta*, No. 2, 1964, p. 13n. (Yakub citing Krylenko and Ya. Berman).
44. *Sotsialisticheskaya Zakonnost*, No. 9, 1966, p. 15 (cited by Strogovich).
45. *Byulleten Verkhovnogo Suda SSSR*, No. 5, 1965, p. 4.
46. *Entsiklopedichesky Slovar Pravovykh Znanii*, p. 245.
47. *Vedomosti Verkhovnogo Soveta SSSR*, No. 1, 1959: Law on Alteration of the Procedure for the Election of People's Courts.
48. *Sovetskaya Yustitsiya*, No. 17, 1966, p. 16.
49. *Vedomosti Verkhovnogo Soveta SSSR*, No. 1, 1959: Bases of Judicial Structure, arts. 31–2.
50. RSFSR *Laws*, 1940, 13: 57.
51. Perlov, *Organizatsiya Raboty Narodnogo Suda*, p. 18.
52. *Sovetskaya Yustitsiya*, No. 17, 1966, p. 17 (Radut-

naya); *Sotsialisticheskaya Zakonnost*, No. 9, 1966, p. 15 (Kurylev).
53. *Sovetskaya Yustitsiya*, No. 24, 1966, pp. 15–16 (Radutnaya).
54. *Ibid.*, No. 2, 1965, p. 2.
55. *Sorok Let Sovetskogo Prava*, pp. 627–8.
56. *Sbornik Deistvuyuschikh Postanovlenii Plenuma Verkhovnogo Suda SSSR*, p. 88.
57. *Izvestiya*, March 27, 1957 (Rakhunov). See also: *Sotsialisticheskaya Zakonnost*, No. 9, 1966, pp. 15–16 (proposal supported by Strogovich, Shafir, Anashkin, Gersaliya and others; opposed by Shubin, Minkovsky and others).
58. *Voprosy Sudoproizvodstva*, p. 66.
59. *Izvestiya*, March 27, 1957 (Rakhunov).
60. *Kommunist*, No. 13, 1961, p. 47 (Burlatsky); Rakhunov, *Uchastniki Ugolovno-Protsessualnoi Deyatelnosti*, p. 115; *Sovetskoye Gosudarstvo i Pravo*, No. 4, 1962, pp. 91–5 (Perlov); *Izvestiya*, May 25, 1962 (unsigned); *Sovetskoye Gosudarstvo i Pravo*, No. 12, 1964, pp. 90–2 (attack on these proposals by Ponedelkov).
61. *Sovetskoye Gosudarstvo i Pravo*, No. 4, 1962, p. 95 (Perlov).
62. *Sotsialisticheskaya Zakonnost*, No. 9, 1966, p. 15 (Zaichuk, Pulatkhodzhaev); *Literaturnaya Gazeta*, March 29, 1967 (Chetunova, reporting Anashkin and others).
63. RSFSR *Laws*, 1918, 26: 420 (347).
64. Karev, *Organizatsiya Suda i Prokuratury*, p. 93.
65. Kursky, p. 66.
66. Piontkovsky and Menshagin, p. 111.
67. *Ibid.*, p. 111.
68. Neishtadt, p. 8.
69. By 1962, 13 out of the 15 Union Republics had passed laws deriving from the 1958 Bases of Legislation on the Judicial Structure (*Sovetskoye Gosudarstvo i Pravo*, No. 3, 1962, p. 57).
70. *Vedomosti Verkhovnogo Soveta RSFSR*, No. 29, 1962.
71. *Sovetskoye Gosudarstvo i Pravo*, No. 10, 1964, p. 4.
72. Feifer, p. 235.
73. *Sovetskoye Gosudarstvo i Pravo*, No. 10, 1965, p. 102 (Shafir).
74. Perlov, *Kak Ustroeny Sud, Prokuratura i Advokatura v SSSR*, p. 87.
75. *Sovetskoye Gosudarstvo i Pravo*, No. 10, 1965, p. 102.
76. *Vedomosti Verkhovnogo Soveta RSFSR*, No. 29, 1962 (Regulatory Order on Defence Lawyers, art. 3).
77. *Sovetskaya Yustitsiya*, No. 1, 1967, pp. 14–15.
78. Regulatory Order on Defence Lawyers.
79. *Sovetskaya Yustitsiya*, No. 14, 1965, p. 26 (Dubkov).
80. Perlov, *Kak Ustroeny Sud, Prokuratura i Advokatura v SSSR*, p. 95.

81. e.g. *Sotsialisticheskaya Zakonnost*, No. 11, 1966, pp. 64–5 (Sinaisky); *Sovetskoye Gosudarstvo i Pravo*, No. 10, 1965, p. 101 (Shafir).

82. *Sovetskoye Gosudarstvo i Pravo*, No. 10, 1965, p. 102 (Shafir).

83. *Sovetskaya Yustitsiya*, No. 22, 1959, p. 22 (Nazarov and Sokolov); *Sotsialisticheskaya Zakonnost*, No. 9, 1960, pp. 25–6 (Karev); *Sovetskoye Gosudarstvo i Pravo*, No. 11, 1960, p. 29 (Samsonov).

84. *Sovetskaya Yustitsiya*, No. 20, 1961, pp. 18–19.

85. *Ibid.*, No. 1, 1958, p. 18; No. 20, 1961, pp. 18–19.

86. *Ibid.*, No. 1, 1958, pp. 15–16.

87. *Izvestiya*, April 8, 1964 (Barkan); *Moskovskaya Pravda*, May 8, 1964 (Osetrov).

88. *Moskovskaya Pravda*, July 1, 1964 (Samsonov); *Sotsialisticheskaya Zakonnost*, No. 5, 1965, p. 79 (Stroev).

89. *Izvestiya*, June 8, 1964 (Boykov).

90. *Sotsialisticheskaya Zakonnost*, No. 5, 1965, pp. 78–80.

91. *Sovetskaya Yustitsiya*, No. 20, 1965, pp. 12–15.

92. *Oktyabr*, No. 5, 1967, pp. 176–7 (Idashkin).

93. *Vedomosti Verkhovnogo Soveta RSFSR*, No. 29, 1962 (Regulatory Order on Defence Lawyers, art. 25).

94. Feifer, p. 234; *Izvestiya*, April 8, 1964; *Sovetskoye Gosudarstvo i Pravo*, No. 10, 1964, p. 12 (Sukharev); *Entsiklopedichesky Slovar Pravovykh Znanii*, p. 140.

95. Details in V. Chornovil's MS *White Book* on 1965–6 trials of Ukrainian nationalists.

96. *Sovetskaya Yustitsiya*, No. 20, 1965, pp. 14–15.

97. Feifer, pp. 234–5; *Sovetskaya Yustitsiya*, No. 18, 1964, p. 7 (Kukarsky).

98. Neishtadt, p. 12.

99. e.g. Lukashevich, pp. 88–89; *Izvestiya*, March 27, 1957 (Rakhunov); and *Sovetskoye Gosudarstvo i Pravo*, No. 6, 1962, p. 120 (Shein); *ibid.*, No. 11, 1966, p. 135, and No. 2, 1967, p. 48 (Shafir); *Sotsialisticheskaya Zakonnost*, No. 1, 1967, pp. 24–25 (Savitsky); *Literaturnaya Gazeta*, September 20, 1966 (Chetunova).

100. *Kommunist*, No. 7, 1956, p. 52 (Rakhunov).

101. *Voprosy Sudoproizvodstva*, p. 451 (proposals put forward by Strogovich, Kaminskaya and Semenkov).

102. Lukashevich, p. 93.

103. *Voprosy Sudoproizvodstva*, p. 296.

104. *Sovetskoye Gosudarstvo i Pravo*, No. 10, 1960, p. 99 (Shatilo), No. 4, 1962, p. 88 (Perlov), and No. 6, 1962, p. 120 (Shein).

105. *Novoye Ugolovnoye Zakonodatelstvo RSFSR*, p. 229.

106. Rivlin, p. 168.

107. (1961) RSFSR Criminal Procedure Code, art. 335.

108. RSFSR *Laws*, 1923, 7: 106.
109. *Sbornik Deistvuyushchikh Postanovlenii Plenuma Verkhovnogo Suda SSSR*, pp. 98–9 (Decision of December 1, 1950, with alterations introduced by decisions of December 4, 1953, and April 10, 1957).
110. Rakhunov, *Peresmotr Prigovorov*, pp. 65–6; *Kommunist*, No. 7, 1956, p. 52.
111. RSFSR Criminal Procedure Code, art. 377.
112. e.g. *Sovetskaya Gosudarstvo i Pravo*, No. 10, 1964, p. 4 (Sukharev).
113. Perlov, *Sudebnoye Sledstviye*, pp. 124–5.
114. e.g. *Sovetskaya Gosudarstvo i Pravo*, No. 5, 1961, p. 71 (Sinaisky *versus* Cheltsov); *Izvestiya*, February 14, 1965 (Perlov *versus* 'individual judges and prosecutors, investigators and scholars').
115. Rakhunov, *Uchastniki Ugolovno-Protsessualnoi Deyatelnosti*, p. 212.
116. *Voprosy Sudoproizvodstva*, p. 202.
117. Raginsky, p. 67.
118. *Voprosy Sudoproizvodstva*, p. 202.
119. Galkin, p. 200.
120. *Sovetskoye Gosudarstvo i Pravo*, No. 5, 1961, p. 74.
121. *Sovetskaya Yustitsiya*, No. 12, 1965, p. 18.
122. Rakhunov, *Uchastniki Ugolovno-Protsessualnoi Deyatelnosti*, p. 223.
123. *Pravda Vostoka*, July 27, 1956.
124. *Izvestiya*, February 12, 1957 (Speech by Kairov).
125. *Byulleten Verkhovnogo Suda SSSR*, No. 6, 1960, pp. 30–2; also *Sovetskoye Gosudarstvo i Pravo*, No. 11, 1964, p. 10.
126. *Sovetskaya Yustitsiya*, No. 7, 1959, p. 21 (Nazarov and Sokolov).
127. *Sotsialisticheskaya Zakonnost*, No. 1, 1967, pp. 26–27 (Savitsky); *Sovetskoye Gosudarstvo i Pravo*, No. 2, 1965, p. 20 (Pankratov) showed that even minors are frequently denied access.
128. Berezovskaya, p. 187.
129. *Izvestiya*, June 8, 1964 (Boykov).
130. RSFSR *Laws*, 1922, 36: 425.
131. Karev, *Organizatsiya Suda i Prokuratury*, p. 84.
132. RSFSR *Laws*, 1923, 10: 120; Lebedinsky and Kalenov, p. 48.
133. USSR *Laws*, 1924, 23: 203; Lebedinsky and Kalenov, p. 47.
134. RSFSR *Laws*, 1926, 25: 624; Lebedinsky and Kalenov, p. 48.
135. USSR *Laws*, 1933, 40: 239.
136. Edict of the Presidium of the USSR Supreme Soviet of May 24, 1955 (*Vedomosti Verkhovnogo Soveta*, No. 9, 1955).
137. Edict of the Presidium of the USSR Supreme Soviet of April 7, 1956 (*Vedomosti Verkhovnogo Soveta SSSR*, No. 9, 1956).
138. A new Regulatory Order on the Military Procuracy was issued in 1966: *Vedo-*

mosti Verkhovnogo Soveta SSSR, No. 50, 1966.

139. *Sovetskoye Gosudarstvo i Pravo*, No. 6, 1964, p. 9; *Sotsialisticheskaya Zakonnost*, No. 4, 1966, p. 13–14.

140. *Sovetskoye Gosudarstvo i Pravo*, No. 1, 1966, p. 135.

141. Lebedinsky and Kalenov, p. 68.

142. Malyarov, p. 45.

143. Lebedinsky and Kalenov, p. 67.

144. *Ibid.*, p. 74.

145. *Ibid.*, pp. 72–3.

146. *Sotsialisticheskaya Zakonnost*, No. 4, 1967, p. 94 (Perfiliev).

147. Lebedinsky and Kalenov.

148. *Ibid.*, p. 85.

149. *Sovetskoye Gosudarstvo i Pravo*, No. 3, 1956, p. 22 (Rudenko).

150. Lebedinsky and Kalenov, p. 75.

151. *Ibid.*, p. 74.

152. Malyarov, p. 320.

153. *Ibid.*, p. 25.

154. *Ibid.*, p. 47.

155. *Sovetskoye Gosudarstvo i Pravo*, No. 2, 1954, pp. 54–5 (Aleksandrov).

156. *Ibid.*, p. 52 (though Galkin, p. 129, assigns this to 1938).

157. *Voprosy Sudoproizvodstva*, pp. 281–5.

158. *Sovetskoye Gosudarstvo i Pravo*, No. 4, 1962, p. 89 (Perlov).

159. *Sovetskoye Gosudarstvo i Pravo*, No. 2, 1957, pp. 40–1 (Barsukov).

160. Galkin, p. 193; and *Sovetskoye Gosudarstvo i Pravo*, No. 4, 1962, p. 89 (Perlov), and No. 9, 1964, pp. 72–73 (Yasinsky).

161. *Voprosy Sudoproizvodstva*, p. 325.

162. RSFSR Criminal Proceduce Code, art. 211; and Tadevosyan, p. 176.

163. RSFSR Criminal Procedure Code, art. 211; and Perlov, *Kak Ustroeny Sud, Prokuratura i Advokatura v SSSR*, p. 65.

164. Tadevosyan, p. 177; also RSFSR Criminal Procedure Code, arts. 63 and 211; and Perlov, *Kak Ustroeny Sud, Prokuratura i Advokatura v SSSR*, p. 65.

165. *Novoye Ugolovnoye Zakonodatelstvo RSFSR*, p. 115; and Rakhunov, *Uchastniki Ugolovno-Protsessualnoy Deyatelnosti*, p. 154.

166. Rakhunov, *Uchastniki Ugolovno-Protsessualnoy Deyatelnosti*, p. 155; and also comparable suggestions in *Sotsialisticheskaya Zakonnost*, No. 6, 1960, p. 62, and *Novoye Ugolovnoye Zakonodatelstvo RSFSR*, p. 115.

167. Lebedinsky and Kalenov, p. 162.

168. Rakhunov, *Uchastniki Ugolovno-Protsessualnoy Deyatelnosti*, pp. 124–5; and *Sovetskaya Yustitsiya*, No. 8, for 1959, p. 57; *Sovetskaya Yustitsiya*, No. 16, 1966, p. 8 (Baskov).

169. *Novoye Ugolovnoye Zakonodatelstvo RSFSR*, p. 164.

170. e.g. *Sotsialisticheskaya Zakonnost*, No. 7, 1965, pp. 5–6 (Zhogin), and No. 8, 1965, p. 56 (Alekseev);

Literaturnaya Gazeta, September 20, 1966 (Chetunova).

171. RSFSR Criminal Procedure Code, art. 22.
172. Ibid., art. 168.
173. Ibid., art. 174.
174. Ibid., art. 205.
175. Sovetskoye Gosudarstvo i Pravo, No. 2, 1954, pp. 59–60 (Aleksandrov).
176. RSFSR Criminal Procedure Code, art. 218 (and Perlov, Sudebnoye Sledstviye, p. 17).
177. Ibid., art 220 (and Tadevosyan, p. 184).
178. Sovetskoye Gosudarstvo i Pravo, No. 2, 1957, p. 42 (Barsukov).
179. Lebedinsky and Kalenov, p. 158; see also Sotsialisticheskaya Zakonnost, No. 7, 1965, p. 21.
180. Izvestiya, November 23, 1966 (Remnev and Temushkin).
181. Voprosy Sudoproizvodstva, p. 74, footnote; Sovetskoye Gosudarstvo i Pravo, No. 1, 1966 (Strogovich versus others).
182. Perlov, Sudebnoye Sledstviye, pp. 103–4.
183. Tadevosyan, p. 202.
184. Perlov, Sudebnoye Sledstviye, pp. 103–12; Tadevosyan, pp. 197–205; and Lebedinsky and Kalenov, pp. 149–55.
185. Voprosy Sudoproizvodstva, p. 128.
186. Tadevosyan, p. 200.
187. Rakhunov, Peresmotr Prigovorov, pp. 14–15.
188. Perlov, Sudebnoye Sledstviye, p. 117.

189. Ibid., pp. 117–18.
190. RSFSR Criminal Procedure Code, art. 335.
191. Ibid., art. 337 (and December, 1958, Bases of Criminal Judicial Procedure, art. 48).
192. See Karev, Organizatsiya Suda i Prokuratury, pp. 182–7.
193. Vedomosti Verkhovnogo Soveta SSSR, No. 12, 1956.
194. Vedomosti Verkhovnogo Soveta SSSR, No. 16, 1956.
195. The first five to do so were: Tadzhikistan (Kommunist Tadzhikistana, November 11, 1958), Georgia (Zarya Vostoka, February 22, 1959), Uzbekistan (Pravda Vostoka, March 26, 1959), Armenia (Kommunist Armenii, April 17, 1959), Kirgizia (Sovetskaya Kirgiziya, April 30, 1959).
196. Karev, Organizatsiya Sovetskogo Suda, p. 183.
197. Perlov, Kak Ustroeny Sud, Prokuratura i Advokatura v SSSR, p. 86.
198. Pravda, June 3, 1956 (Decree of the Central Committee of the CPSU and the USSR Council of Ministers of May 30, 1956).
199. Entsiklopedichesky Slovar Pravovykh Znanii, p. 509.
200. Dobrovolskaya, pp. 134–139.
201. See Izvestiya, May 18, 1958, and Ugolovnoye Zakonodatelstvo RSFSR, p. 157, for contrasting points of view.

202. *Sotsialisticheskaya Zakonnost*, No. 9, 1966, pp. 13–14 (many lawyers); *Izvestiya*, January 4, 1967 (Dorgeev).

203. *Sovetskaya Yustitsiya*, No. 22, 1966, pp. 10–11 (Vasiliev; *see* also *Komsomolskaya Pravda*, October 9, 1966 (Lalayan).

III
Criminal Procedure

———※———

Soviet criminal procedural legislation covers three main stages: the preliminary investigation; the trial; and appellate jurisdiction.

PRELIMINARY INVESTIGATION

The type of preliminary investigation carried out before a case is taken to court is determined by the nature of the crime. For petty offences such as minor hooliganism, preliminary investigation as such is not required and the conduct of an 'inquiry' (*doznanie*) by the militia is all that is necessary for instituting court proceedings. (It has been suggested at a high level that 'this institution is increasingly losing its significance' and should be done away with.[1]) At the other end of the scale the preliminary investigation in cases of treason, espionage, terrorism, sabotage, wrecking, anti-Soviet agitation and propaganda, the organisation or commission of especially dangerous State crimes and mass disorder is handled by the Committee of State Security (KGB).[2] Between these two extremes, the investigation of all other crimes is initiated by the militia and carried on by the investigators attached to the Prosecutor's Office or by those subordinate[3] to the Ministry for the Protection of Public Order. Low investigating standards are the subject of official complaint;[4] one reason is a high turnover of investigators.[5]

Suspects can be detained by the militia or the investigator only when the offence committed may attract a sentence of deprivation of freedom (i.e. in prison or in a corrective labour colony) and provided that either the suspect was caught in the act, or that witnesses directly testify to his having committed the crime, or that traces of the crime are revealed upon him or on his clothing.[6] If none of these requirements is met, a suspect can be detained only in the event of attempting to escape, having no permanent domicile, or of his identity being unestablished. Sanction for the suspect's detention in custody must be obtained from the prosecutor within 48 hours.[7]

[55]

If there is reason to believe that the offender may seek to escape trial, or may hinder the establishment of the truth, or may engage in criminal activity, preventive measures may be applied by the investigator, the prosecutor or the court.[8] These include: a written undertaking not to leave the place of domicile, the obtaining of sureties from third parties, and preventive detention.[9] In exceptional circumstances, such measures can be applied before any charge has been preferred, but not more than ten days must elapse before this is done.[10] Preventive detention can be applied only in cases where a sentence of deprivation of freedom may be passed, though in respect of grave crimes its application is permissible on the sole ground of the danger of crime.[11] The maximum standard term for preventive detention is two months; this can be extended in cases of a particularly complex nature to three months by regional prosecutors, and by the Prosecutor of a Union Republic or the Chief Military Prosecutor up to six months. Any further extension has to be sanctioned by the USSR Prosecutor-General and may not exceed nine months in all.[12]

There are many shortcomings in pre-trial practice, quite apart from the anomalous position occupied by the prosecutor in pre-trial proceedings. Investigation, it has been said, is often subject to an incriminatory trend,[13] insufficient attention is paid to the accused's explanations;[14] and defence lawyers are by no means present at all the preliminary investigations which they are entitled to attend. During 1964, the figure for attendance was a mere 8–10 per cent of such cases (not including those where attendance was obligatory). One reason was the unsatisfactory explanation to the accused of his rights.[15] Cases where minors have not been permitted to see defence counsel —a gross violation of the procedural code—are frequent.[16]

It is certain that the investigator has relatively wide scope for manœuvre before preferring a definite charge and so conferring the status of 'accused' upon the presumed offender. The status of 'suspect' has been retained as a procedural form in the RSFSR Code of Criminal Procedure in the face of considerable debate.[17] Yet the practice whereby persons detained as suspects were, under certain circumstances, interrogated as 'witnesses' with all the consequent penalties for giving false testimony, which gave rise to great injustice for many years,[18] has now, it is said, been disavowed.[19] What still is a regressive factor is the tendency to identify the fact that the accusation has been proceeded with as an inferential assumption of the guilt of the accused; as one of the liberal Soviet jurists revealingly remarked on the eve of the legal reforms:

'Soviet laws provide all the necessary procedural guarantees against unjustified prosecution or arrest. But even under these conditions it happens that not every person who is prosecuted is guilty.'[20]

This assumption that only the guilty are brought to trial and that the court has only to assess the gravity of the crime still persists at least in the minds of some prosecutors and investigators and is the subject of continued controversy.[21] One local assistant prosecutor went as far as to write to the Soviet Press alleging that:

'The law gives the organs of investigation the right to prefer charges against one or other person and to question him as the accused and thus deem him guilty. The prosecutor commits for trial and prosecutes a person who is already guilty from the point of view of the organs of investigation, e.g. from the point of view of the authorities.'[22]

The dangers of this attitude are all the greater in the light of the admission that 'quite a few so-called "speculative" cases still come before the courts'. Here the prosecutor and investigator are not sure of how well founded the charges are themselves, but do not stop the cases going forward. At other times

'one can also often see cases which are sent before the courts because the investigator and the prosecutor have not found the courage to say that the case should be stopped either because of lack of evidence or because the real criminal should be found'.[23]

COURT PROCEEDINGS

Preparatory session. Up to December, 1958, all criminal cases bearing an indictment by a prosecutor had first to be presented at a preparatory session of the court in question,[24] but this requirement has since been modified to provide for the holding of preparatory sessions only where the judge is in disagreement with the act of indictment or where the preventive measure (detention, etc.) applied to the accused needs to be altered.[25] This is in most respects a retrograde step save in that of expediting the process of law. Earlier experiments with making preparatory sessions optional had been discontinued in 1934 as 'unsatisfactory'.[26] Previous rulings and comments had firmly endorsed the value of the preparatory session: as a 1934 Decision of the Plenum of the USSR Supreme Court had stated, the best means of ensuring that judges did check up properly on the thoroughness, well-foundedness and correctness of the indictment before the hearing was the holding of a preparatory session:

'if this responsibility is laid solely upon the judge, it is not in fact attended to as practice has shown, and this gives rise to a high percentage of unfounded court trials'.[27]

Under the present RSFSR dispensations, preparatory sessions, when held, are attended by the court chairman and two people's assessors and the prosecutor is now obliged to take part in them.[28] This session has a number of important functions: it decides whether or not to institute court proceedings; whether or not to alter the charge preferred; and whether, under article 18 of the Criminal Procedure Code, the trial should be held in camera.[29]

Trial. First-instance hearings of cases, as distinct from appellate hearings, take place at all levels of the court system, from the People's Court up to the USSR Supreme Court. The bulk of cases, both criminal and civil, are dealt with in the People's Courts. Courts have been recommended to assign not fewer than 18–20 days a month to judicial hearings.[30] Fixed periods are laid down within which cases assigned to the court must come up for trial, ranging, according to the category into which they fall, from one month to five days. The accused and his defence counsel have the right to challenge the investigator, prosecutor or judge(s) trying the case on certain procedural grounds, such as being related to one of the parties, having an interest in the outcome of the case, having participated as a witness, etc.[31] Witnesses are liable to a punishment of up to six months' corrective labour for refusal to testify.[32]

The All-Union legislative enactments of December, 1958, encouraged Soviet jurists to weed out a number of retrogressive procedural anomalies relating to trial procedure. This process had gone quite far in the RSFSR. The establishment by the court of the order of proceedings no longer hinges on whether the accused has pleaded 'guilty' or 'not guilty',[33] as used to be the case.[34] The court is no longer entitled to omit further interrogation if the accused recognises his guilt and confesses,[35] an absolute anomaly to which Soviet lawyers had earlier drawn attention.[36] The same fate has overtaken the outdated provision whereby an *oblast* court acting as a court of first instance might refuse to allow the customary speeches by the parties to the case.[37]

The procedural drawbacks met with in practice are varied: the giving of less weight to the oral evidence of the accused than to that of the witnesses;[38] the influence exerted by the moral character of the accused on the court's assessment of the evidence;[39] refusal to allow justified requests for the replacement of investigators or prosecutors;[40] investigators giving too much credence to the testimony of experts;[41] trial in absentia.[42] However, so far as trial in a regularly constituted court of law is concerned, the indications are that such procedural miscarriages are few and becoming fewer. This does not mean they do not occur: one eminent Soviet authority has repeatedly drawn attention to the grave consequences attendant on 'judicial errors' and to the existence of theorists who even consider that the defence is a hindrance to the discharge of their duties by the court and the investigation.[43]

APPELLATE PROCEDURE

Appellate jurisdiction and procedure occupy a prominent place in the Soviet legal system. There are two main types of appellate procedure—cassational and supervisory. The former covers all cases where the sentence has not entered into force; the latter where it has. Cassation procedure takes two forms: 'protests' by the appropriate levels of the Prosecutor's Office to higher courts (i.e. courts of second instance), and 'appeals' lodged by defendants or their lawyers with higher courts. Supervisory appellate procedure is not available to defendants or their counsel but only to the appropriate official instances within the Prosecutor's Office and to the chairmen of all courts down to regional level; it cannot therefore be initiated by 'appeals' but only by 'protests' from one or other prosecutor or court. There is also a third, lesser-used form of appellate procedure available to the Prosecutor's Office—the review of sentences in connection with 'newly-discovered circumstances'.

Cassation. All sentences by all courts other than those of the USSR Supreme Court and the Supreme Courts of the Union Republics may form the subject of a cassation protest or appeal.[44] (It has been suggested that the Supreme Courts of the

[59]

Union Republics should not enjoy this exemption, all the more so in that they often have to function as first instance courts,[45] but this has evidently met with opposition on the grounds that

'The freedom of protest against sentences and decisions should not be regarded as a precept which is subject to no limitations.'[46]

Nevertheless, lawyers continued to urge that sentences passed by republican Supreme Courts be liable to cassational procedure. They differed, however, in their views as to whether the cassational instances in these cases should be the USSR Supreme Court or the Presidium of the Union Republic's own Supreme Court.[47] Evidently there was a feeling that the 'sovereignty of the Union Republics' was at stake.[48])

The grounds on which cassation protests or appeals may be lodged are:[49]

(1) One-sidedness or incompleteness of the preliminary investigation or the court proceedings;
(2) non-conformity of the court's findings to the factual circumstances of the case;
(3) significant infringement of the rules of criminal procedure;
(4) incorrect application of criminal law;
(5) non-conformity of the sentence passed to the gravity of the crime and the character of the condemned person.
(These grounds also govern the lodging of supervisory protest.)

Cassation protests and appeals against a court of first instance are to be heard by the next higher court;[50] for this reason the People's Courts have no cassation jurisdiction, and the presidium of any given court of first instance is not entitled to exercise a cassation review of the findings of its own court. While cassation appeals by the accused must be reviewed in court, cassation protests submitted by a lower prosecutor can be annulled by a higher prosecutor before they appear for review in court.[51] Both appeals and protests must as a rule be delivered within a week after the verdict of the court of first instance.[52]

The court reviewing the cassation appeal does not re-try the case; it does not re-establish the objective truth of the initial findings but checks on the attainment of it by the court of first instance.[53] At the same time, its review is not confined to the points listed in the protest or appeal, but covers the whole of the preceding investigatory and judicial proceedings.[54] Since the reviewing court does not re-examine the actual evidence, though the accused may, at the court's discretion, be allowed to attend it,[55] he must confine himself in any oral evidence he may volunteer to 'giving explanations' (i.e. refrain from adducing new evidence). New evidence may be submitted to the court but it must be in written form.[56]

The court reviewing cassation appeals or protests can do one of four things: confirm the original verdict; set it aside and order a re-trial; set it partially aside and alter it; set it aside and terminate proceedings.[57] If a partial amendment is decided upon by the reviewing court without any submission for retrial, this can only be to reduce the severity of the punishment or reclassify the crime under a less severe heading.[58]

At the cassation hearing the prosecutor's position is somewhat peculiar. He is variously regarded by Soviet jurists as still a party to the case[59] or as no longer one.[60] When presenting a protest emanating from a lower prosecutor, he is acting in the interests of the prosecution as well as in his other capacity of supervisor of legality; when appearing in a review arising from an appeal by the defence, the prosecutor, being *ipso facto* in agreement with the judgment of the court of first instance, is said to be 'exercising his functions of supervision over the exact execution of Soviet laws'.[61] Alternatively, it is argued that he must be impartial, is not bound by the findings of the junior prosecutor and can take the defence's side where no new documents have been produced by them.[62] (The junior prosecutor sometimes has the invidious task of having to support a decision by his superior to which he has already shown himself to be opposed.[63]) The fact that the views of Soviet lawyers diverge sharply on this question largely reflects the uncertainty provoked by the bifocal nature of the prosecutors' duties in this as in other stages of judicial proceedings. There must in any case be a presumption that the prosecutor is under some obligation to pay 'special attention to cases in which the courts have acquitted or have terminated proceedings',[64] since the very fact of a judgment of this sort being recorded runs counter to the fact of a prosecution having been instigated at all; and the prosecutor must therefore conclude either that the acquittal is unjustified or that his own investigators were initially at fault, and take appropriate action.[65] A recent textbook warned against 'one-sidedness' and 'bias' in initiating a protest 'merely because the court did not agree with the original position of the prosecutor who appeared in court'.[66]

The results of a survey carried out in 1965–66 showed that 'intervention by the prosecutor is clearly insufficient': cassation protests by prosecutors were only made with regard to 11·7 per cent of the sentences subsequently recognised as being incorrect by the courts themselves.[67] In 1953, 6·6 per cent of all cassation reviews were at the instigation of the procuracy; by 1963, this figure had dropped to 3·8 per cent.[68] Nor do the practices of the courts give grounds for optimism:

'Mistakes made by the courts should be corrected at once, that is by cassation procedure; sometimes this is far from the case, however. The Saratov regional court, apparently striving for stability in court decisions, leaves sentences unchanged at the cassation stage but the same sentences are revised at the supervisory stage. We do not need the stability of every court decision, but only the just ones.'[69]

Yet the authorities' emphases on the importance of 'stability'[70] suggest why courts strive to achieve this state even to the detriment of legality.[71]

Old attitudes towards appeals by defendants and lawyers die hard. Court officials

'who see an intriguer or a litigious person behind every appeal still exist, and a defence lawyer is sometimes considered to be a person who tries to save his client . . . at any price'.[72]

Supervisory Procedure. Supervisory procedure differs from cassation procedure in that no general limit is set for its initiation, save that it cannot be lodged until the sentence has acquired legal force. Within this proviso, there can be different dispensations. In the RSFSR supervisory protests against sentences of conviction on the grounds of leniency of punishment or the need to apply the sanctions provided for a more serious crime must be lodged within a year from the sentence taking legal effect and likewise in respect of all protests against sentences of acquittal.[73] Whereas the defence can initiate cassation appeals to a higher court, supervisory protests can be initiated only by prosecutors or court chairmen, and the defence can only make representations to the prosecutor that he should take such action.[74] Moreover, a supervisory review checks not only on the findings of the court of first instance but also on all cassation proceedings, and any previous supervisory reviews that may already have been heard.[75]

[62]

While, as with cassation procedure, supervisory protests are, as a rule, reviewed in the next higher court, strict continuity does not have to be observed if the obtaining of a general authoritative ruling is deemed necessary, or speed of procedure is desirable.[76] Thus a supervisory protest entered against the verdict of a regional court can on occasion be reviewed by the USSR Supreme Court. It was, indeed, to deal with the situation where the USSR Supreme Court was overloaded with appellate procedure from lower courts that a law of August 14, 1954,[77] set up presidiums for all regional courts and Supreme Courts of Union Republics and Autonomous Republics, thus enabling them all to function as supervisory instances. Even so, it was evidently some time before this had the desired effect, for, as the Deputy Chairman of the Supreme Court of the USSR noted in July, 1957,[78] the by-passing of intervening instances had continued after 1954 and resulted in a sharp increase in the membership of the Supreme Court, which had already reached a total of 79 at the elections in 1951.[79] However, by 1957 a sharp reduction had taken place, the Supreme Court membership falling from 79 to 12 and the number of its people's assessors from 35 to 20.[80]

The right of supervisory protest was strictly regulated in April, 1955.[81] The USSR Prosecutor-General, the Chairman of the USSR Supreme Court and their deputies, can lodge protests with the presidium of any court; the Prosecutor and Supreme Court chairman of a Union Republic and their deputies with the presidium of any court in that republic; all regional prosecutors down to *oblast* level with the presidiums of all regional courts. Just as People's Courts do not have any supervisory jurisdiction, so district prosecutors do not have any right of supervisory protest. Supervisory protests against the verdicts of People's Courts are normally heard at *oblast* level. A further step in reducing the load on the USSR Supreme Court was the decree of February, 1957,[82] confining the right of protest by the USSR Prosecutor-General against appellate decisions of the Presidiums of Union Republic Supreme Courts to cases where these conflict with All-Union legislation or the interests of the Union Republic; a similar clause was introduced in respect of protests against first-instance decisions by the same courts.[83] In due course, however, the wheel came full circle and there were complaints about the 'excessive contraction of supervisory functions [which] deprive the USSR Suppreme Court of the possibility of acting as the highest supervisory organ'.[84] The USSR Supreme Court Plenum is the highest of all the appellate instances and is the only one entitled to review protests against the collegiums of the USSR Supreme Court.

The parties to the action are not as a rule present at supervisory protest hearings though in the RSFSR and other republics the court may now summon them to attend at its discretion;[85] the attendance of the prosecutor in obligatory.[86] Decisions are taken by a simple majority of votes. No members of the court presidium who have participated in previous hearings of the case can take part in the supervisory hearings; if, as can sometimes occur at *oblast* level where the membership of the court presidium may total four to five in all,[87] the majority of the members have so participated, the review is transferred to the next higher court (this will also in fact apply in cassation hearings by such courts).

One of the principal distinctions between cassation and supervisory procedure is the treatment of the principle of *reformatio in pejus*. From at least 1950 to 1957, despite the embodiment of this principle in Article 26 of the pre-1958 Bases of Criminal Judicial Procedure,[88] a cassation court could, when reviewing an appeal submitted by the accused, order a re-trial on the grounds of the leniency of the original sentence, and the sentence against which the defendant had protested could be increased on re-trial if new facts came to light or a law involving more severe punishment needed to be applied by the re-trial court.[89] (If, however, the cassation action arose from a protest by the prosecutor, the question of *reformatio in pejus* did not, of course, arise.) This ruling of December, 1950, appears to have been modified in April, 1957,[90] and was certainly amended the following year[91] to disenable the cassation court from ordering a re-trial on the grounds of too mild a sentence, where the appeal was lodged by the accused. However, this does not rule out the possibility (envisaged in an earlier ruling of February, 1940[92]) of the cassation court making representations to higher courts possessing supervisory jurisdiction about the need for increasing the sentence. A lawyer has admitted that

'convicted persons, as well as defence lawyers, sometimes avoid cassation appeals against sentences, although they consider them to be severe or incorrect . . . They fear that as well as turning down their cassation appeal, the collegium would add a rider . . . about the leniency of the sentence and a protest by the court chairman at the leniency . . . might be introduced. In the practice of the Moscow City Court there have been occasions when sentences have been altered because of their leniency on account of protests by the court's chairman, at the same time as these cases have come to court with appeals against the severity of the punishment.'[93]

In addition, the court of re-trial can still increase the punishment if new circumstances are uncovered revealing the commission of a more severe crime, even where the re-trial arose from a protest by the accused.[94] Since no supervisory reviews directly arise from appeals by the accused, the principle of *reformatio in pejus* in relation to a re-trial ordered by supervisory instances does not apply. Indeed, as already noted, supervisory courts have the right under certain circumstances to review sentences of acquittal up to one year from their taking effect;[95] the danger of abusing this facility has not passed unremarked.[96]

Soviet lawyers have argued[97] that there is a particular need for defence representation at supervisory reviews in view of the fact that if the protest has been initiated by the court chairman, who also presides over the hearing, he has already, in effect, taken sides against the accused.[98] In practice, defence counsel had been admitted to such hearings until 1940, when the People's Commissariat of Justice pointed out that this usage had no legal basis.[99] In addition, it has been customary for the accused to be uninformed of the fact of his case being under review and only to hear of it after the event, if at all.[100] In fact a slight change for the better was made in December, 1958, when it was laid down that the supervisory court had the 'right where necessary to summon the accused to attend the court hearing'.[101] Soviet lawyers have also continued to advocate that provision be made for the notification of the accused of the impending re-examination of his case to enable him to take action on his own behalf.[102]

There has been criticism of the way in which a court presidium conducting a supervisory hearing makes its decision in public, in contrast to cassational practice where a collegium meets behind closed doors. The presidium decision is taken

'in the presence of the prosecutor, the person who gave the report (often not a presidium member) and other people (who are giving reports on other cases). Before the resolution is pronounced, the prosecutor frequently persuades presidium members what sort of decision should be made. If the prosecutor or chairman of a regional court sees that the majority of presidium members is against the supervisory protest, it is dismissed.'

The critic went on to disparage the undue importance of the person delivering the report in this procedure[103] (who may be the court chairman or a member of the presidium or court designated by him who has not taken any previous part in the case[104]).

Several authorities have expressed concern at the 'extreme undesirability' of the rise in protests at the supervisory stage at the expense of cassation protests. In 1963, compared to 1953, the percentage of supervisory protests by prosecutors rose from 30·8 to 73·3 while cassation protests dwindled from 69·2 to 26·7.[105] The experience of the Moscow City Court in recent years has shown that over a third of all previous court sentences and rulings are quashed or altered at the supervisory protest stage in the year after they have come into effect.[106]

'NEWLY-DISCOVERED CIRCUMSTANCES' PROCEDURE

The final form of appellate jurisdiction is what is called 'review of sentences on the basis of newly-discovered circumstances'.[107] This form is in all major respects an extension of the super-visory protest procedure which it resembles as regards the limitations imposed on the defence, the courses of action open to the court of review, and the method established for the consideration of evidence. The features specific to it are the grounds for its initiation; the procedure for its initiation; and the period during which it can be lodged. Thus the grounds for reopening the case in this way must be grounds of which the previous court or courts were unaware when passing sentence. They are: false evidence on which the sentence was based; criminal abuse of their functions by the judges who delivered the judgment; and other freshly ascertained circumstances proving the innocence of the accused or his participation in a crime more or less serious than that for which he was sentenced.[108]

The procedures outlined in the various Republican Codes for its initiation include substantial divergences but are largely in agreement that it is the prosecutor who does so. Though RSFSR regulations provide for citizens, organisations generally and officials (including presumably the accused, his defence lawyer, or his relatives) to be able to petition for a review, such petitions take effect only through the intermediacy of the prosecutor.[109] All representations by the prosecutor on the subject have to be directed to the next higher court to the court of first instance in the given case.[110] An important feature is the time limits imposed: these again vary somewhat between republics, but the generally adopted rule is for such reviews of all verdicts of acquittal to be heard not later than one year from the discovery of new circumstances and not later than five years from the entry into force of the verdict, save where the grounds for action are false witness or abuse of their functions on the part of the judges.[111] The review of sentences of conviction is not subject to a time limit. This form of appellate jurisdiction is no doubt rarely met with, but Soviet sources indicate that it is used and has resulted (*qua* re-trial direction) in the increase of sentences[112] as well as in their reduction.

SOURCES

1. *Sovetskoye Gosudarstvo i Pravo*, No. 6, 1965, p. 10 (Tikunov).
2. December, 1958, Bases of Criminal Judicial Procedure, art. 28; and *Vedomosti Verkhovnogo Soveta SSSR*, No. 26, 1961, p. 615.
3. Edict of the Presidium of the USSR Supreme Soviet of April 6, 1963 (*Sovetskoye Gosudarstvo i Pravo*, No. 9, 1964, p. 69).
4. *Sotsialisticheskaya Zakonnost*, No. 4, 1966, pp. 9–16 (reference to 1965 Decree on improving investigatory work); *ibid.*, No. 1, 1967, p. 11 (Zhogin).
5. *Ibid.*, No. 4, 1966, p. 10; *Sovetskoye Gosudarstvo i Pravo*, No. 11, 1966, p. 44 (Chugunov and Gorsky).
6. RSFSR Criminal Procedure Code, art. 122.
7. *Ibid.*, art. 122.
8. *Ibid.*, art. 89.
9. *Ibid.*, arts. 93–6.
10. *Ibid.*, art. 90.
11. *Ibid.*, art. 96.
12. *Ibid.*, art. 97.
13. *Sovetsky Ugolovny Protsess*, p. 125; *Sovetskoye Gosudarstvo i Pravo*, No. 6, 1965, p. 6 (Tikunov); *Sovetskaya Yustitsiya*, No. 16, 1966, p. 8 (Baskov).
14. *Sovetsky Ugolovny Protsess*, p. 125, and *Sotsialisticheskaya Zakonnost*, No. 7, 1960, pp. 12–16 (Urakov).
15. *Sotsialisticheskaya Zakonnost*, No. 1, 1967, pp. 26–28 (Savitsky).
16. *Sovetskoye Gosudarstvo i Pravo*, No. 2, 1965, p. 20 (Pankratov).

17. Galkin, pp. 204–5.
18. *Sovetsky Ugolovny Protsess*, pp. 143–4; *Sorok Let Sovetskogo Prava*, pp. 620–1; Lukashevich, pp. 120–1 and 116–17; and Galkin, pp. 220–1.
19. *Novoye Ugolovnoye Zakonodatelstvo RSFSR*, p. 106; and RSFSR Criminal Procedure Code, art. 76.
20. *Kommunist*, No. 7, 1956, p. 48 (Rakhunov). Similar sentiments were ascribed to Mokichev (*Kommunist*, No. 14, 1959, p. 122—review by Kudryavtsev).
21. *Literaturnaya Gazeta*, August 18, 1964 (Filimonov and Strogovich); *Izvestiya*, September 9, 1964 (Chaikovskaya); December 2, 1964 (Gorkin).
22. *Literaturnaya Gazeta*, August 18, 1964.
23. *Sovetskaya Yustitsiya*, No. 16, 1966, p. 8 (Baskov).
24. Perlov, *Organizatsiya Raboty Sovetskogo Suda*, p. 79.
25. RSFSR Criminal Procedure Code, art. 221.
26. *Sovetskoye Gosudarstvo i Pravo*, No. 2, 1959, p. 59 (Golunsky).
27. *Sbornik Deistvuyushchikh Postanovlenii Plenuma Verkhovnogo Suda SSSR*, p. 80 (Decision of June 7, 1934, with alterations introduced by decisions of May 8, 1941, and December 4, 1953); *see also* pp. 85–8 (Decision of September 15, 1950, with alterations introduced by decisions of January 9, 1953, and September 13, 1957).
28. RSFSR Criminal Procedure Code, art. 224.
29. *Ibid.*, arts. 226–8.
30. Perlov, *Organizatsiya Raboty Sovetskogo Suda*, p. 92.
31. RSFSR Criminal Procedure Code, arts. 59–64.
32. RSFSR Criminal Code, art. 82.
33. *Novoye Ugolovnoye Zakonodatelstvo RSFSR*, p. 140.
34. Perlov, *Sudebnoye Sledstviye*, pp. 72–90.
35. *Novoye Ugolovnoye Zakonodatelstvo RSFSR*, p. 140.
36. *Sorok Let Sovetskogo Prava*, p. 632.
37. *Novoye Ugolovnoye Zakonodatelstvo RSFSR*, p. 142.
38. Perlov, *Sudebnoye Sledstviye*, p. 161.
39. *Ibid.*, p. 164.
40. Neishtadt, pp. 23–4.
41. *Ibid.*, p. 27.
42. *Zarya Vostoka*, March 15, 1956.
43. *Literaturnaya Gazeta*, May 23, 1964 (Strogovich).
44. RSFSR Criminal Procedure Code, art. 325; and *Novoye Ugolovnoye Zakonodatelstvo RSFSR*, p. 158.
45. *Sovetskoye Gosudarstvo i Pravo*, No. 4, 1962, pp. 92–3 (Perlov); and *Sovetskaya Yustitsiya*, No. 6, 1962, p. 14 (Perlov).
46. Dobrovolskaya, p. 72.
47. *Sotsialisticheskaya Zakonnost*, No. 9, 1966, pp. 12–13 (Koblikov, Perlov, Sha-

menov supported widening of USSR Supreme Court's powers).

48. *Ibid.*, p. 13 (Strogovich).

49. December, 1958, Bases of Criminal Judicial Procedure, art. 49; and Rivlin, pp. 170–1.

50. RSFSR Criminal Procedure Code, art. 326; and Rakhunov, p. 18.

51. RSFSR Criminal Procedure Code, art. 326; Tadevosyan, p. 146; Lebedinsky and Kalenov, pp. 57 and 170.

52. RSFSR Criminal Procedure Code, art. 328.

53. Rivlin, pp. 58–9; *Sovetskoye Gosudarstvo i Pravo*, No. 4, 1962, p. 91 (Perlov); and RSFSR Criminal Procedure Code, art. 332.

54. Rivlin, p. 57; and RSFSR Criminal Procedure Code, art. 332.

55. Under arts. 409–10 of the previously valid RSFSR Criminal Procedure Code (RSFSR *Laws*, 1923, 7: 106) the defendant had to be given prior warning of a cassation hearing by the court and was entitled to attend it; under the December, 1958, enactments (art. 45 of the Bases of Criminal Judicial Procedure) and the 1961 RSFSR Criminal Procedure Code (art. 335) it is the court that rules on whether the defendant may attend the court hearing. This has evidently been the subject of some controversy, e.g. *Voprosy Sudoproizvodstva*, p. 464, and *Sovetskoye*

Gosudarstvo i Pravo, No. 12, 1964, p. 93 (Ponedelkov).

56. RSFSR Criminal Procedure Code, arts. 337–8.

57. *Ibid.*, art. 339.

58. *Ibid.*, art. 340; and Rivlin, p. 221.

59. Rivlin, p. 155.

60. Lebedinsky and Kalenov, p. 170; and Rakhunov, *Uchastniki Ugolovno-Protsessualnoi Deyatelnosti*, pp. 171–3.

61. Rivlin, p. 156.

62. Rakhunov, *Uchastniki Ugolovno-Protsessualnoi Deyatelnosti*, pp. 171–2.

63. *Sovetskoye Gosudarstvo i Pravo*, No. 10, 1965, p. 48 (Baskov).

64. Lebedinsky and Kalenov, p. 167.

65. *Ibid.*

66. Malyarov, p. 189.

67. *Sovetskoye Gosudarstvo i Pravo*, No. 11, 1966, p. 41 (Chugunov and Gorsky).

68. *Byulleten Verkhovnogo Suda*, No. 5, 1964, p. 4 (Kulikov).

69. *Ibid.*, No. 4, 1965, p. 5 (Malyarov).

70. e.g. *ibid.*, p. 4.

71. *Sovetskaya Yustitsiya*, No. 22, 1966, p. 10 (Vasiliev).

72. *Ibid.*, No. 9, 1966, p. 2.

73. RSFSR Criminal Procedure Code, art. 373.

74. Neishtadt, p. 33.

75. RSFSR Criminal Procedure Code, art. 379.

76. Rakhunov, *Peresmotr Prigovorov*, p. 50.

77. Edict of Presidium of USSR Supreme Soviet of August 14, 1954 (*Vedomosti Verkhovnogo Soveta,*

No. 17, 1954); and *Novoye Ugolovnoye Zakonodatelstvo RSFSR*, p. 33.

78. *Sovetskoye Gosudarstvo i Pravo*, No. 7, 1957, p. 24.

79. *Pravda*, March 13, 1957.

80. *Pravda*, February 13, 1957.

81. *Vedomosti Verkhovnogo Soveta SSSR*, No. 7, 1955.

82. Decree of the Presidium of the USSR Supreme Soviet of March 29, 1957 (*Vedomosti Verkhovnogo Soveta SSSR*, No. 8, 1957).

83. *Ibid.*

84. *Sotsialisticheskaya Zakonnost*, No. 9, 1966, p. 13 (Perlov); *Sovetskaya Yustitsiya*, No. 18, 1965, p. 23 (Zimner).

85. RSFSR Criminal Procedure Code, art. 377.

86. December, 1958, Bases of Criminal Judicial Procedure, art. 48; and Lebedinsky and Kalenov, p. 173; and RSFSR Criminal Procedure Code, art. 337.

87. Rakhunov, *Peresmotr Prigovorov*, p. 9.

88. USSR *Laws*, 1924, 24:206 (Decree of the All-Russian Central Executive Committee of October 31, 1924).

89. *Sorok Let Sovetskogo Prava*, p. 639; Perlov, *Sudebnoye Sledstviye*, pp. 32–3; Kutsova, p. 166.

90. *Sorok Let Sovetskogo Prava*, p. 640 (refers to Decision of Plenum of USSR Supreme Court of April 10, 1957).

91. RSFSR Criminal Procedure Code, arts. 340–1.

92. Rivlin, p. 255; Kutsova, p. 164 (refers to Decision of Plenum of USSR Supreme Court of February 10, 1940).

93. *Sovetskoye Gosudarstvo i Pravo*, No. 10, 1965, p. 48 (Baskov).

94. December, 1958, Bases of Criminal Judicial Procedure, art. 52; and *Novoye Ugolovnoye Zakonodatelstvo RSFSR*, p. 156.

95. RSFSR Criminal Procedure Code, art. 373.

96. *Sovetskoye Gosudarstvo i Pravo*, No. 8, 1962, p. 65 (Maslov).

97. e.g. Rakhunov, *Peresmotr Prigovorov*, pp. 64–6; Rivlin, pp. 236–8 and 255–6; *Kommunist*, No. 7, 1956, p. 52 (Rakhunov).

98. e.g. Rakhunov, *Peresmotr Prigovorov*, p. 64.

99. *Ibid.*, p. 65 (referring to Order No. 29 of the People's Commissariat of Justice of the USSR dated March 25, 1940).

100. *Ibid.*

101. December, 1958, Bases of Criminal Judicial Procedure, art. 48; and RSFSR Criminal Procedure Code, art. 377.

102. *Sovetskoye Gosudarstvo i Pravo*, No. 8, 1962, p. 57 (Maslov).

103. *Sotsialisticheskaya Zakonnost*, No. 9, 1965, pp. 11–12 (Datsenko); *see also*: *Sovetskaya Yustitsiya*, No. 23, 1965, p. 13 (Komissarov); *Sovetskoye Gosudarstvo i Pravo*, No. 10, 1965, p. 50 (Baskov).

104. RSFSR Criminal Procedure Code, art. 377.
105. *Sovetskaya Yustitsiya*, No. 23, 1965, p. 12 (Komissarov); *Byulleten Verkhovnogo Suda SSSR*, No. 5, 1964, p. 4 (Kulikov); *ibid.*, No. 4, 1965, p. 5 (Malyarov); *Sovetskoye Gosudarstvo i Pravo*, No. 10, 1965, p. 45 (Baskov); Malyarov, p. 189.
106. *Sovetskoye Gosudarstvo i Pravo*, No. 10, 1965, p. 45 (Baskov).
107. Lebedinsky and Kalenov, p. 176; Rivlin, pp. 261–274.
108. RSFSR Criminal Procedure Code, art. 384.
109. *Ibid.*, art. 386.
110. *Nauchno - Praktichesky Kommentarii UPK RSFSR*, pp. 711–13.
111. RSFSR Criminal Procedure Code, art. 385; and Rivlin, pp. 265–6.
112. Rivlin, p. 267.

IV

Crime and Punishment

Perhaps the only constant in the whole field of Soviet legal theory over the 50 years and more that it has existed has been the explanation it puts forward of the existence of crime in a Socialist society. Now, as in 1917, there is still a tendency to attribute this to the 'vitality of capitalist survivals in the consciousness of a certain section of Soviet citizens',[1] though the premise of the 'presence of capitalist encirclement' has been finally discarded. Nevertheless, for several years, there have been many indications that this explanation is deemed inadequate on its own. Attention is now also paid to the 'internal factors' supporting these vestiges of capitalism;[2] the influence of such things as consumer goods shortages, alcoholism, parental absence in wartime[3] and even 'material difficulties of poorly-paid sections of workers'[4] is acknowledged. The significance of sociological factors has been recognised[5] and one source has recommended a quintuple classification under:

(a) family upbringing;
(b) school upbringing;
(c) mass-cultural upbringing;
(d) everyday environment;
(e) material deficiencies.[6]

The fact remains that for Soviet theorists while crime under capitalism is a 'genuinely irrevocable social phenomenon engendered by the very nature of a monstrous social system',[7] under Socialism crime is deemed to be an alien phenomenon. Already in 1936, when with the completion of the first phase of development of the Soviet State the liquidation of all exploiting classes was completed, the norms of Soviet law were deemed to express not the will of the working class on its own but the will of the entire Soviet society, consisting of the two 'friendly' classes of workers and peasants, and also the intelligentsia.[8] More recently, in the Party Programme adopted at the XXII Congress of the CPSU the transition from a State of the dictatorship of the proletariat to a State of the entire people was formally proclaimed. In accordance with this, Soviet law is said to derive its mandate from 'the inner agreement of the overwhelming majority of the members of society with the prescripts of Soviet Socialist legal norms'.[9]

Yet the possibility of dispensing with law and, its corollary, of totally eradicating crime, has still not yet been the subject of any authoritative formulation. It is still an article of faith that:

'In a developed Communist society (where the necessary external factors—the victory and consolidation of socialism on a world scale —exist) law will die away.'[10]

Yet the November, 1961, Party Programme, which deals in detail with the transition to such a society, patently avoids any forecast in its scanty and lame comments on Soviet law and the way ahead. The eventual substitution of voluntary moral compliance for legal compulsion is at present to be achieved by a two-fold drive in diametrically opposed directions: the application of even greater penal coercion to the unregenerate few together with the communal re-education and regeneration of the redeemable majority of offenders (*see* Chapter V). This has led, on the one hand, to the introduction of more rigorous judicial sanctions and, on the other, to the by-passing of the judiciary in favour of various forms of community action.

The fight against 'capitalist survivals' is an unquestionably urgent one in the eyes of the Soviet authorities; the premises from which they proceed are shaky. By the beginning of 1966, three-quarters of the Soviet population was born after 1917.[11]

It is by no means the case that crime is confined to the quarter or so of the population born before the Revolution. From figures relating to the presence of defence counsel during preliminary investigations, it can be deduced that in 1964 about 15 per cent of cases which reached court involved minors or defendants physically or mentally handicapped.[12] Although attempts have been made to stress that many lawbreakers are idlers and parasites[13] or young people neither working nor studying,[14] other authorities affirm that 'working youth' forms by far the largest section of young criminals.[15] Among the administrative actions taken which reflect anxiety about lawlessness among the young is the imposition of curfews.[16] Faced with this situation, the theoreticians can only weakly assert that 'remnants of the past' affect young people also.[17] The fact that one of the commonest (discovered and undiscovered) forms of offence involves theft of Socialist property[18] does little to improve the ideological picture.

The object of Soviet justice, as formulated in December, 1958,[19] is to protect from infringement:

(a) The public and State system of the USSR, the Socialist economy and Socialist property;

(b) the political, labour, housing and other rights and interests of citizens;

(c) the legally protected rights and interests of State enterprises, collective farms, co-operatives and other public organisations.

Similarly, the object of Soviet criminal law is the 'protection of the Soviet public and State system, and Socialist property, of the persons and rights of citizens and of the entire Socialist legal order from criminal infringements'.[20] It is the attainment of these objects that determines, or should determine, the definition of norms of crime, and of the criteria and aims of punishment.

Without full rule of law, without true conceptual differentiation between public and private interests, and with what is essentially an emphasis on the regenerative rôle of law, it cannot be said that Soviet law and justice always incorporate in practice or in theory the meaning generally attached to these two terms.

DEFINITION OF CRIME

As was indicated in the introductory section, few consistent attempts were made in the first two decades after the Revolution to define the nature of crime in objective legal terms. All sorts of obstacles, both practical and theoretical, got in the way. The earliest criteria were largely discretional ones bound up with the 'revolutionary legal consciousness' exercised by the judiciary and other interested authorities. At a later stage, when normative acts were resorted to, such a definition as these provided was always dependent upon the extra-judicial powers and procedures that existed alongside, and often in direct contradiction to, these acts. On the theoretical plane, the existence of the institute of analogy* and the drafting of

* See p. 138.

very widely-drawn *corpora delicti* perpetuated the discretionary elements. On the procedural plane, quite apart from the special procedures introduced to deal with counter-revolutionary activity, the rulings on evidence, confession, the definitions of intent, complicity and so-called 'objective truth' also made for wide latitude in the establishment of criminal liability. Moreover, the conception of guilt was deemed to be integrally bound up not only with the social danger of the crime but with the socially dangerous character of the criminal. It is still the case that the elaboration and equation of the dual concepts of 'social danger' and 'illegality' give rise to a great deal of confusion. Since, by its own definition, Soviet law embraces almost the whole field of relations between individuals and corporations, including administrative and economic law, while all infringements of law are socially dangerous, not all of them are criminal. The question therefore arises of whether the compilers of criminal law must be deemed responsible for covering the question of social danger in framing *corpora delicti*, or whether the courts must pronounce not only on the presence of crime, as defined in the attributes and criteria of a given *corpus delicti*, but also on the question of social danger. In the first case, the corollary is the need for legislators to frame an all-embracing set of *corpora delicti* characterised by explicit 'definitions' ('dispositions'). In the latter, the tendency will be toward less well-defined, 'generic' *corpora delicti* with wider 'definitions' in which the question of social danger will have to be decided upon by the court as an attribute of the crime alongside other material attributes.[21] The All-Union principles of December, 1958, did not go unreservedly in the direction of the first trend. They provided, for example, that

'activity or inactivity, though formally carrying the attributes of some action covered by criminal law, yet not constituting a social danger by virtue of its insignificance, is not a crime.'[22]

In other words, the notion of social danger was still an integral element for ruling on a *corpus delicti* and, moreover, in certain circumstances, a notion to be defined not by the legislator but by the court. However, the first trend, which appears to be supported by the majority of Soviet criminal lawyers,[23] has made progress. In the 1961 RSFSR Criminal Code a large number of the *corpora delicti* have been framed with explicit definitions in which some though not all of the possible criteria establishing social danger are specified.[24]

In recent times the provision for the prosecution of, and actions for the redress of offences against, individual citizens in their non-official capacity have been tightened. It remains true that State interests are wide and the notion of social danger is likewise extensive. However broadly or narrowly defined, the sort of actions that attract criminal prosecution range over a very wide field. Apart from infringements of the regulations concerning Government or Socialist property, which, *per se*, is all property not in private hands, such actions as the manufacture of sub-standard goods or the pursuit of various forms of trading, or the resale of goods can enter into the category of criminal actions.

Nor is the actual commission of a crime by any means a prerequisite for prosecution. Soviet legislation still provides for considerable latitude in the definitions as 'criminal' of the preparation for or an attempt to commit a crime; of complicity in, instigation of, or connivance at, a crime; of the concealment of a criminal, and of failure to report a crime.

ASSESSMENT OF GRAVITY

The legal assessment and the socio-political assessment of crime are deemed inseparable. As has been remarked:

'When it is a question of the cognition of truth in court, the phenomena of objective reality constituting the contents of this truth are established in their legal and in their interrelated social-political essence, and it is completely impossible to divide this cognition into the cognition of the phenomena as such and the cognition of their essence, just as it is to subtract from the conception of the truth established in court the legal and social-political essence of the facts constituting the sum of it.'[25]

It is the socio-political essence of the assessment of a crime, which, over and above its material attributes, is used, whether by the legislator or by the courts, to determine its degree of gravity. Thus the order of listing anti-State crimes in Soviet criminal law has always been, and still is, framed in terms of the relative danger they constitute to 'basic State interests, to the bases of the public and State system, to the bases of the State administration of the USSR'.[26] Thus the order of compilation of the Special Section of Criminal Law, governing such crimes, 'is not a technical but a political question—the question of the assessment of various crimes from the point of view of the interests of the Soviet State and the policy it conducts'.[27] (Now that the Union Republics regularly issue their own Codes such curious discrepancies emerge as the fact that in 12 of the republics' recent Criminal Codes five different definitions of particularly dangerous recidivism 'are to be met with'.)[28]

The relative degree of social danger, and hence of the gravity of a crime, may depend upon other considerations than the immediate attributes of the relevant *corpus delicti*.[29] Severe consequences resulting from the crime, even if only indirectly, so long as there is some causal link, have a bearing upon its qualification.[30] The frequency of a given crime in a given area is also a relevant factor; thus the theft of grain in a collective farm where there have been similar occurrences before may, it is said, be treated more severely than in a collective farm where this has not previously occurred.[31] The rarity, rather than the face value, of stolen property is among the criteria which may determine the exact qualification of the form of theft.[32] It has been considered necessary, however, in present-day theory and court-room practice, to establish quantitative criteria for thefts, e.g. those involving sums of 10,000 roubles or over are regarded as being 'particularly large'.[33] Nevertheless, these are not 'mechanical "limits"' and practice has shown that qualitative criteria may decide border-line cases to the defendants' disadvantage.[34] As the death penalty is applicable, for example, where 'particularly large' thefts are involved (see below), the lack of precise legal definition is disturbing. The personal character of the accused in terms of his social danger is also a criterion for determining the punishment to be awarded.[35] As has been said:

'Individualisation of punishment in Soviet criminal law is a principle consisting in taking into account the character and degree of social danger of the guilty party and the aggravating and mitigating circumstances.'[36]

Other social criteria that increase the gravity of an offence are the 'utilisation of religious and national prejudices'.

DEFINITION OF PUNISHMENT

Both the December, 1958, Bases of Criminal Legislation and the new RSFSR Criminal Code state:

[77]

'Punishment not only constitutes chastisement for the crime committed but also has as its aim the correction and re-education of condemned persons in the spirit of an honest attitude to labour, exact compliance with law, respect for the rules of Socialist communal order, and also the prevention of the commission of new crimes by the accused as well as by other persons. Punishment does not have the aim of causing physical suffering or the lowering of human dignity.'[37]

The Soviet theoretical view of punishment, leaving aside the question of its implementation in practice, has undergone a considerable change since the earliest years of the Revolution, when it was thought of as a necessary evil, having as its object the terrorisation and suppression of the enemies of the Revolution. The concept of terrorisation did not, on the theoretical plane, survive the end of the Civil War (though there are even now odd references to it still being an 'element' in punishment[38]) and was overtaken by that of re-education. However, the relative importance of the two remaining constituent elements of chastisement and correction is even now the subject of disagreement. The view that chastisement (i.e. suffering) was an aim, as distinct from an attribute, of punishment appears to have been largely discarded—the question is rather where correction ends and only chastisement remains.

One school of thought is said to view punishment as solely a pedagogic process.[39] Others maintain that chastisement is a synonym for punishment and that the civic reclamation of the criminal is something separate though concomitant. They add that the term 'forced labour' is no longer applicable save in the case of an insignificant minority, and should be considered not punitive but re-educative.[40] Others took the view that the element of 'chastisement', or even 'retribution', was, on the contrary, not only an actual object of punishment but also, in long sentences, its sole object.[41] There is, none the less, no tendency to deny the preventive significance of punishment as a by-product of the element of chastisement[42] (although it was admitted in 1965 that the 'basic question' of the effectiveness of punishment was unresolved by the available statistics[43]), and penal sanctions are also held up as 'contributing to the education of all citizens in a spirit of hatred for socially harmful and dangerous "birthmarks" of the past'.[44] Prevention is regarded as vital for the minority still prone to crime, but the 'effectiveness of punishment consists not in its severity, though

[78]

in certain cases the most severe punishment is needed as a preventive measure. The effectiveness of punishment consists in its inevitability'.[45] If criminal sanctions were abolished crime would grow.[46]

Participants in a recent discussion, who voiced different shades of opinion on the nature of punishment, came to the general conclusion that the aims of punishment should be formulated more clearly in order to guide judges and prosecutors. This view was given additional point by the statement, made by one of those present, that a quarter of his charges in a place of confinement considered that they had been dealt with very harshly, having failed to understand that 'it was the law, not the judge, that had punished them'.[47] A foreign student of the Soviet legal scene has suggested that judges do not have rehabilitation at the forefront of their minds when sentencing those found guilty.[48]

A further important feature of Soviet justice as a preventive and corrective institution is what may be called the concept of communal condemnation. As one prominent authority has written:

'Court examination and the condemnation of the criminal constitute not only prevention in respect of morally unstable persons; they show up, in all their ignominy, before citizens persons who betray the duty of a Soviet citizen, who violate Socialist property—thieves, speculators, hooligans, etc.—and teach citizens a clear understanding of the damage caused the State and society by criminals, a deeper understanding of the justness of Soviet law, a surer grasp of the interests of the State, and teach them to heighten their own vigilance.'[49]

(This concept of communal condemnation is dealt with in Chapter V, pp. 115–125.)

(This concept of communal condemnation is dealt with in Chapter V, pp. 115–125.)

OLD AND NEW PUNISHMENTS

Under the December, 1958, dispositions, punishments that can now be applied are:[50]

(1) deprivation of freedom;
(2) banishment;
(3) deportation;
(4) corrective labour without deprivation of freedom;
(5) deprivation of the right to occupy certain posts or pursue a given employment;

(6) fine;

(7) public condemnation.

Supplementary punishments are confiscation of property and deprivation of military or other rank. Of those listed above, (1), (2), (5) and (6) can figure as supplementary as well as basic punishments. Union Republics may fix other forms of punishment, in conformity with the general principles enunciated in December, 1958. (The 1961 RSFSR Criminal Code follows the All-Union disposition very closely.[51]) Finally, execution by shooting is listed as an 'exceptional measure' applicable to certain anti-State crimes and, in other cases where specified, 'until the time of its full abolition'; it may not be applied to those under 18 or to pregnant women.[52]

The Death Penalty. There is nothing new about the 1958 formulation looking forward to the 'total abolition' of capital punishment which is repeated word for word in the RSFSR Criminal Code of 1961. The death penalty has several times been introduced and abolished in the Soviet Union. But formal abolition of it has not prevented its application when the occasion demanded.

The imposition of the death penalty at the front was abolished in October, 1917;[53] in February, 1918, its reimposition by the Cheka was announced[54] and in June, 1918, implicitly extended to the Revolutionary Tribunals.[55] In January, 1920,[56] it was again abolished, followed by its implicit reintroduction in May, 1920.[57] In subsequent years, various decrees either restricted or extended its use, until it was again formally abandoned on May 26, 1947,[58] to mark the attainment of complete security against internal and external foes. Despite this, ostensibly in response to public demand, it was reintroduced in January, 1950, for traitors, spies and saboteurs,[59] and extended in April, 1954, to cover cases of deliberate murder in aggravating circumstances.[60]

Further extensions were decreed in 1961–62,[61] notably to cover:

> (May, 1961) particularly large-scale theft; counterfeiting; violence by prisoners in places of detention.
>
> (July, 1961) foreign currency offences.
>
> (February, 1962) attacks on militiamen or people's guards.
>
> (February, 1962) aggravated rape.
>
> (February, 1962) aggravated bribery.

So that far from the December, 1958, and subsequent dispositions being a retreat, they are, in fact, a marked advance on the
post-1950 ones. The new RSFSR Criminal Code still looks
dauntlessly forward to the 'total abolition' of the death
penalty.[62] Published direct criticism of the continued existence
of the death penalty is very rare, but at least one writer has
described the (still applicable) post-1961 extensions as 'a result
of the voluntaristic and subjective [i.e. Khrushchevian] approach, condemned by the Party'.[63]

Banishment and Deportation. Banishment (*ssylka*), which
dates back to 1922,[64] involves expulsion from the place of residence, and forced settlement in another specified locality; it is
said to 'deprive the condemned person of freedom of movement and so reduce his degree of social danger'.[65] Deportation (*vysylka*), which dates back to 1923,[66] involves expulsion
from the place of residence and a ban on residence in specified
areas. At that time, the maximum period formally applicable
for either was three years; in 1930 it was raised to 10 years for
banishment and five years for exile.[67] Under the December,
1958, provisions the maximum period for either, whether as a
basic punishment or as a supplementary one, has been lowered
to five years.[68] There has recently been one authoritative call
for a more extensive use of banishment to cover such offenders
as hooligans, illegal distillers and speculators.[69]

Deprivation of Freedom. Deprivation of freedom covers
both incarceration in prison and detention in any one of the
corrective labour colonies with régimes of varying severity
(four for men, two for women, and three for male and one
for female delinquents under 18 years old[70]).

After the Civil War, during which no legal limit had been
laid down for periods of deprivation of freedom, the official
maximum rose from five years in 1921 to 10 in 1922 and, later,
to 25 years in 1937. It has now been reduced to 15 years for
'specially dangerous recidivists' and in cases specially provided
for, with a maximum of 10 years in all other cases and for those
under 18.[71] For 'grave crimes', and for 'specially dangerous
recidivists', the whole or part of the sentence may take the
form of incarceration in prison.[72] Equally, persons detained in
corrective labour colonies may be transferred to prison for up
to three years for infringing the corrective labour régime.[73]

The court may pass a conditional sentence of deprivation of
freedom, i.e. the sentence is not put into effect provided the

accused commits no further offence during the period of probation specified in the verdict.[74] For those actually serving a sentence, remission can be earned by 'good conduct and an honest attitude to work' while the sentence is being served.[75] The system of remission has, however, been tightened up, both in its formal enactment and in its practical application. Current legislation specifically excludes specially dangerous recidivists from any remission of sentence.[76] Persons convicted of 'grave crimes' must serve two-thirds of their sentence before becoming eligible for remission, and all other prisoners one-half of the sentence.[77] Simultaneously, enforcement of the law was tightened up and the practice followed by the corrective labour authorities of allowing one 'work-day' to count for two to three days of the sentence to be served was abolished. Release had to be on the basis of a court decision and not on the basis of administrative action by the corrective labour authorities.[78]

Deprivation of freedom used until a few years ago to be the most important and widely used form of punishment.[79] But the indications are that, save in the case of the graver crimes, this form of punishment is being less widely employed.[80]

Corrective Labour without Deprivation of Freedom. There has been little change in this form of punishment. The maximum sentence continues, as in 1922,[81] to be one year.[82] This form of labour is performed either at the offender's place of work or at other enterprises in the area where he is living. Up to 20 per cent of earnings may be deducted.[83] It would appear that this continues to be one of the most widely used forms of punishment.

Confiscation of Property. This measure can only be applied as a supplementary punishment where specifically provided for, as is now, for example, the case with speculation in foreign currency.[84] Current RSFSR legislation (which more or less follows that originally enacted in the early 1930s) totally exempts from confiscation only articles of domestic use, while any sums of money and foodstuffs left unconfiscated need not exceed the monetary equivalent of a month's salary for each member of the family.[85]

Punishment of Juveniles. A turn for the better has taken place in the criminal liability of juveniles. Since December, 1958, criminal liability has been raised from 14 to 16 except for major crimes (murder, bodily injury, rape, assault and battery, malicious hooliganism, large-scale theft, deliberate destruction of property, and deliberate action liable to lead to a train smash) for which the age of liability has been raised from 12 to 14.[86] (Yet there is a certain amount of inconsistency between the Codes of the Union Republics, in some of which certain forms of theft are punishable at 14, not 16.[87])

At the same time, though these provisions mark an advance on the hitherto valid enactment of April 7, 1935,[88] establishing the age of criminal liability for major crimes at 13, and of May 31, 1941,[89] at 14 for these and all other crimes, they do not restore the pre-1922 position, when minors under 18 were *a priori* subject to criminal liability but were dealt with by a special Commission for Minors.[90]

As regards forms of punishment, the death sentence cannot be applied to those aged under 18.[91] This appears to be an advance on the post-1933 position, when, despite conflicting laws and rulings, this possibility was not entirely excluded. For those under 18 the maximum term of deprivation of freedom may not now exceed 10 years,[92] and they may not be sentenced to either banishment or deportation.[93]

Frequently the age of juveniles is not established. This sometimes involves illegal arrests.[94] In 1966 a case came to light in which a 12-year-old schoolgirl had been charged with theft.[95]

Old Punishments. 'Enemy of the Toilers', 'Outlawry', and 'Enemy of the People'—these three punishments have now been dispensed with; they appear, in any case, to have been in disuse for a number of years.

Outlawry is encountered in a decree of November 26, 1917, in relation to the leaders of the White armies.[96] Both it and the designation of 'enemy of the Revolution or the People' were incorporated into the first RSFSR Criminal Law Principles of December 12, 1919,[97] without any explanation of their content. Deprivation of citizenship (which first cropped up in December, 1921[98]) and expulsion from the USSR in perpetuity (first specified in the 1922 RSFSR Criminal Code[99]) became in 1924 consequential upon being declared an enemy of the toilers, for crimes 'threatening the bases of the Soviet régime'.[100] Outlawry, in turn, was first given a precise content in a retroactive law of November 21, 1929,[101] invoking it in all cases of refusal on the part of Soviet officials abroad to obey a recall to the USSR, and making confiscation of property and shooting contingent upon it.

The term of 'enemy of the people' appears to have last found specific legal application in a law of August, 1932,[102] applying very severe sanctions in case of thefts of collective farm property—and the fact of its being so employed led, as has been subsequently admitted, to the impossibility of incorporating this law into the Criminal Code, as well as contributing to 'large-scale infringements of Socialist legality'.[103] Though obsolescent, all three designations continued to be enumerated in post-Stalinist legal textbooks.[104]

Deprivation of Electoral Rights. The December, 1958, dispositions retain certain forms of deprivation of civil rights such as the right to occupy certain posts or engage in a given line of activity; they abolish the deprivation of electoral rights.[105] However, the previous formula of deprivation of 'political rights' provided in Article 31 of the RSFSR Criminal Code extended only to electoral rights, the right to occupy elective posts in public organisations and to occupy specified official posts. The December, 1958, wording appears to retain the latter two elements of deprivation of 'political rights'. As regards the non-deprivation of electoral rights, this is perhaps more a concession to constitutional appearances than anything else, since the deprivation of them can in few cases constitute any practical hardship.

CRIMINAL RECORD

Soviet law institutionalises the state of having a criminal record (*sudimost*); if further offences are not committed within a specific period whose length depends on the original court sentence (which may not even be one of deprivation of liberty), this record is automatically expunged—except in the case of those sentenced to 10 years or more of deprivation of liberty, when a court decision is required.[106] In post-1958 legislation, provision has been made for this state of having a criminal record to be expunged prematurely 'at the request of public organisations' in the light of the 'exemplary behaviour and honest attitude towards work' of the person involved.[107] A recent legal reference work indicates what this post-penal stage involves:

'When a new crime is committed, having a criminal record is an aggravating circumstance and in certain cases serves as a basis for acknowledging a person to be a particularly dangerous recidivist. The existence of the criminal record may lead to the restriction of residence to defined areas, to preventing the occupation of certain posts, to depriving the person of the opportunity to occupy himself in one activity or another.'[108] *See* p. 125 for *ex post facto* legislation.

COUNTER-REVOLUTIONARY AND ANTI-STATE CRIMES

The notion of counter-revolution has never been far below the surface in Soviet law. Well after the end of the Civil War, after the period of War Communism, after the effective strait-jacketing of the inner-Party opposition, it continued to dominate the scene. Quite apart from the treason trials that were engineered on and off throughout the 1930s, its influence on legislative activity was harmful in the extreme. The USSR Supreme Court ruling of January 2, 1928, directed that counter-revolutionary offences were present

'when the person who committed them, although not directly pursuing a counter-revolutionary aim, wittingly entertained the possibility of this arising or should have foreseen the socially dangerous character of the consequences of his actions'.[109]

This opened the door to prosecution on counter-revolutionary charges not merely in the case of indirect intent but even in that of careless actions.[110] Indeed, already in 1929 the RSFSR Supreme Court was noting a tendency to attach a political colouring to purely mundane cases.[111] The law of August 7, 1932, on the protection of State property introduced the application of the death penalty for a very wide range of offences, and the courts appear to have been invited to extend it still further in practical application.[112] The same tendency towards increasing the severity of repression and devising special procedural measures to cover what were regarded as counter-revolutionary crimes was evident in the laws of December 1, 1934,[113] and September 14, 1937,[114] establishing virtually extra-judicial procedures in such cases. Connected with this was 'the tendency which received extremely wide application in judicial practice to view the maximum laid down by law in the context of relative sanctions as a minimum for the purpose of the practical administering of punishment in any given case'.[115] Even the December 31, 1938,[116] ruling of the Plenum of the USSR Supreme Court, which purported to clear up the vexed question of 'intent', merely limited itself to the formula of 'where it is established by the circumstances of the case that the accused acted with a counter-revolutionary aim'; this was

[85]

both disingenuous and tautological, for the offences covered by this ruling already listed 'counter-revolutionary aim' among the attributes of the *corpus delicti*. What neither the ruling nor the *corpora delicti* provided was any orientation on 'direct' and 'indirect' intent. Even in 1957 there were still said to be supporters among Soviet lawyers of the application of 'indirect intent' to counter-revolutionary crimes.[117]

At the present time the position is somewhat improved. The two procedural laws of 1934 and 1937 referred to earlier have been repealed; the maximum penalties for counter-revolutionary crimes have been generally reduced; analogy has been dispensed with; and 'indirect intent' has, in the opinion of many Soviet legal writers, been deemed inapplicable,[118] though this point of view is rejected by the USSR Supreme Court.[119] But there still remains some lack of definition. Though the December, 1958, Law on State Crimes has eliminated the former classification of State crimes into 'counter-revolutionary crimes' and 'crimes against the administrative order of especial danger to the USSR' in favour of the two headings 'especially dangerous State crimes' and 'other State crimes', this is a terminological change:[120] the December, 1958, *corpora delicti* are modelled very closely on their predecessors (as are also the derivative Republican Criminal Codes).

ESPECIALLY DANGEROUS STATE CRIMES

(a) *Treason to the Fatherland*[121]

Definitions ('dispositions'):

Defection to the enemy;
Espionage;
Disclosure of State secrets to a foreign power;
Flight abroad or refusal to return from abroad;
Affording of assistance to a foreign power in carrying on hostile activity against the USSR;
Conspiracy for the seizing of power.

Sanction:

Ten to 15 years deprivation of freedom with confiscation of property and with or without banishment of two to five years,[122] or the death penalty with confiscation of property (previously lower limits ranged variously, from three to 10 years).

The definitions included in this article represent an amalgamation of various articles in the old Criminal Code. It is noteworthy that no distinction is made between servicemen and civilians, or between officials and private persons, for the article starts 'action deliberately committed by a citizen of the USSR to the detriment of the State independence, the territorial inviolability or the military might of the USSR'. Thus it not only covers the 1929 law[123] on the non-return from abroad of government employees and the 1934 law[124] on the flight of servicemen abroad, but also retains the 1934 provision[125] in respect of ordinary civilians, whether abroad on work or otherwise, provided they engage in or intend to engage in hostile activity.[126]

Moreover, the concept of 'defection to the enemy' is treated in certain Soviet textbooks as capable of extension beyond the physical sense, including 'direct contact with the enemy, service with the enemy, desertion to the enemy in wartime, abandonment of USSR citizenship', wartime 'participation in treasonous nationalist bands',[127] or, for example, serving the enemy in an administrative capacity in wartime,[128] or even 'crossing the front line ... and also surrendering into enemy captivity in certain cases'.[129]

As regards 'flight abroad' a distinct but belated correction is the abandonment of that part of the law of July 20, 1934,[130] which made the adult members of the family of any servicemen defecting or attempting to defect abroad automatically responsible for his action. Even as late as 1955 it was repeated that such persons were liable to 'banishment to remote parts of Siberia for a period of five years' even if they had not contributed to, or even known of the escape; and that

'the political significance of it consists in the strengthening of the overall preventive action of the criminal law for the purpose of averting so heinous a felony as the action of a serviceman in crossing or flying across the frontier, as a result of which the guilty party cannot himself be subjected to punishment'.[131]

It is hardly to be wondered at that one Soviet source, even before its annulment, described this provision as a 'foreign body in current legislation'.[132] At the same time, in respect of the serviceman (or civilian) himself, it would appear, failing any more specific definition, that, as was stated in a 1958 textbook, his defection 'is treason to the Fatherland irrespective of whether any further concrete activity in the enemy's interests followed on his part. The very fact of defection or flight abroad already constitutes from the objective point of view the *corpus delicti* of treason to the Fatherland.'[133]

Moreover, his family may still, under the December, 1958, definition of 'complicity',[134] be exposed to prosecution as 'co-participants'; or as 'accessories' if they have no more than 'contributed to the commission of the crime by giving advice, instructions, providing resources or removing obstacles'. A 1958 authority assigned to the category of complicity the preparation of food or help with packing on the part of the defector's relatives.[135] Flight abroad specifically includes defections while on a 'business or tourist visit'. Direct intent can be shown merely by a request for political asylum. However, if the defection is 'on material grounds' or is to another Socialist State (!) this comes under a less severe heading.[136]

There is a clash of opinion among lawyers as to whether treason can only be committed with direct anti-Soviet intent or not. A recent textbook took issue with exponents of the 'direct intent' view, asserting that liability could also be incurred through indirect intent.[137]

Espionage as a treasonable activity is governed by a decree of the USSR Council of Ministers of April 28, 1956,[138] establishing definite categories of State secrets, both military and economic. It has been stated that

'for espionage to be present it is not required that data constituting a State secret should have been transmitted to foreign States, counter-revolutionary organisations or private persons. Espionage is considered completed at the stage when data constituting a State secret have been stolen or assembled ... Espionage is considered completed when the recruitment of persons for espionage is performed and also when consent has been given to engage in espionage activity.'[139]

In addition espionage also extends to the collection or transmission, etc., at the instigation of a foreign intelligence, of 'other data': these can be 'published or unpublished data about various aspects of policy, economy, defence, science, technology and culture of the USSR'; they might even include published or unpublished information about 'registration procedure in hotels, procedure for sending baggage across the State frontier, market prices of consumer goods', or 'about oil reserves'. The storing of such data can also qualify under this heading.[140] One authority suggests that even 'information about customs and the local peculiarities of individual areas of the USSR' could be qualified as espionage.[141] One major amendment has, however, been introduced, notably the 1960 law which frees from criminal liability any USSR citizens recruited by foreign intelligence services who refrained from carrying out any assignment and voluntarily confessed.[142] The KGB authorities have claimed that this law was drafted at their suggestion.[143]

Espionage committed by a foreign or a Stateless person has now been listed separately and is punishable by a sentence of from seven to 15 years and confiscation of property, or by the death penalty and confiscation of property.[144] Conspiracy to seize power was the main charge against Beriya.[145]

A recent textbook disagreed with one of its predecessors and claimed that espionage can be committed with indirect intent.[146]

(b) Terrorist Acts[147]

Definition: Murder of a State or public official or an official representative committed in connection with his State or public activity, with the aim of weakening the Soviet régime.

Sanction: From 10 to 15 years deprivation of freedom with confiscation of property and with or without banishment of from two to five years, or the death penalty with confiscation of property (previous lower limit—three years). In the event of the infliction of severe bodily injury, the sanction is reduced to eight to 15 years with confiscation of property and with or without banishment of from two to five years.

The basic legislation defining the objects of terrorist acts dates from 1922;[148] its terms of reference were thereafter rapidly broadened. The potential objects of terrorist acts came to include worker correspondents and rural correspondents (1924); communal teachers (1929); members of the auxiliary grain procurement commissions (1930); shock-workers (1931); and pioneers (1934);[149] and it, by definition, includes all Party officials. Formerly relatives of such officials could also constitute the object of terrorist attacks[150] but current legislation eliminates such a widened interpretation of the term.[151] Similarly, damage to property apparently no longer provides grounds for the charge[152]—such provision had in fact been introduced by the USSR Supreme Court in 1931 at the time of the mass liquidation of the *kulaks*. Currently it can certainly cover 'rank and file employees of State institutes', and 'rank and file members of public organisations (Party, Komsomol, public, TU, etc.) as well as the people's militia, members of comrades' courts, etc.'.[153] It has been suggested that the clause should cover attempts on the lives of 'progressive public men from Capitalist States in USSR territory'.[154]

Direct anti-Soviet intent must, it has been stated,[155] be present in the commission of a terrorist act. A terrorist act cannot apply when the offence against the victim is committed from personal hostility, or for motives of gain. If no coercive action has in fact taken place, the offence may be that of an attempt at, or preparation of, a terrorist act.[156]

Terrorist acts against representatives of a foreign State 'in the aim of provoking war or international complications' are listed as a separate category.[157] The sanctions for them are exactly the same.

(c) Wrecking[158]

Definitions:

Destruction or damage by explosion, arson or other means of enterprises, installations, transport facilities and communications or other forms of State or public property;

Mass poisoning or the spreading of epidemics and epizootics—in either case with the aim of weakening the Soviet State.

Sanction:

From eight to 15 years deprivation of freedom with confiscation of property and with or without banishment of from two to five years, or the death penalty with confiscation of property (previously, lower limit—three years).

Wrecking (*diversiya*) is distinguished from sabotage (*vreditelstvo*) in that it can have only Socialist property (factories, railways, schools, etc.) as its object as distinct from the workings of the economic system; and is normally an isolated act or acts (demolition, shipwreck, etc.) as distinct from a continuous process. The 'other means' referred to in the definitions may, it has been said, 'take the form of spoiling of rolling stock, damage to agricultural machinery, etc.'[159]

The charge of wrecking figured in most of the purge trials throughout the 1930s; in the 1950s it was stated that 'the danger of wrecking for the Soviet State has not lapsed even at the present time',[160] and post-war cases are cited, of which one supposed example was the alleged American use of bacteriological warfare during the Korean war.[161] * For a charge of wrecking, it is not necessary that the act of wrecking shall have been completed,[163] equally, where there has merely been preparatory activity, a charge of attempted wrecking applies.[164] It is differentiated from other similar destructive actions by the presence of a direct counter-revolutionary aim, as distinct from personal motive or motives of hooliganism.[165] Prosecutions, however, are said to have occurred in practice where only 'indirect' counter-revolutionary aim was in question.[166]

(d) Sabotage[167]

Definition: Activity or inactivity directed towards the undermining of industry, transport, agriculture, the credit system, trade and other branches of the national economy and also at the functioning of State organs or public organisations with the aim of weakening the Soviet State, if pursued by means of utilising State or public institutions, enterprises, organisations, or by opposing their normal work.

Sanction: From eight to 15 years deprivation of freedom with confiscation of property and with or without banishment of from two to five years (previous lower limit: three years (*qua* 'activity'), one year (*qua* 'inactivity')).

Sabotage (*vreditelstvo*), unlike wrecking, does not necessarily involve physical destruction, nor does it take the form of a single localised act; it usually has an element of continuity to it, such as 'for example, incorrect planning, the creation of difficulties in matters of supply, the disorganisation of production, etc.'.[168] It may 'extend over a whole branch of the economy, e.g. the coal-mining industry'.[169] It is, however, not

* In 1966 V. Kochetov, a writer renowned for his conservative attitudes, implied that the Americans were responsible for spreading epidemics such as cholera and foot-and-mouth disease (an outbreak of which was affecting the Soviet Union at the time).[162]

necessarily limited to the economic plane but may be reflected in any field of Socialist construction, education, health, justice, medicine, etc.;[170] the December, 1954, trial of the former Minister of State Security, Abakumov, included a charge of sabotage.[171]

The preferment of this charge, which was first given definite formulation in 1922[172] but rephrased in 1923,[173] was at its height during the late 1920s and early 1930s *vis-à-vis* the old technical intelligentsia and the *kulaks*; but as a recent work has stated:

'Sabotage as a means of struggle against the Soviet State has not lost its danger at the present time ... The reactionary forces of imperialist States openly assign vast sums in order to dispatch wreckers, saboteurs and murderers into the USSR.'[174]

Sabotage is present from the moment of the offender—who may work in a 'public organisation'[175]—utilising his post or job to this end, irrespective of the attainment of any consequential result.[176] But it is distinguished from offences such as crimes by officials, to which it bears a similarity, by the presence of direct counter-revolutionary intent.[177] It presupposes direct anti-Soviet intent.[178]

The present definitions cover both 'activity' and 'inactivity', thus combining in one article what was previously covered separately, by Articles 58[7] and 58[14] of the previous RSFSR Criminal Code.[179]

(e) Anti-Soviet Agitation and Propaganda[180]

Definitions:

Agitation or propaganda conducted with the aim of undermining or weakening the Soviet régime or of committing individual specially dangerous State crimes;

The propagation, with this aim, of slanderous distortions, calumniating the Soviet State and public régime;

The distribution, preparation or keeping for these aims of literature of the aforesaid content.

Sanction: From six months to seven years deprivation of freedom, with or without banishment of from two to five years, or banishment of two to five years without deprivation of freedom. Also, if committed by a person previously condemned for specially dangerous State crimes or committed during wartime, the sanction is from three to 10 years, with or without banishment of from two to five years.*

Agitation is usually in relation to a wide circle of persons; propaganda in relation to a narrow or defined circle of persons. Not only the preparation and retention of anti-Soviet literature, which may be leaflets, books or placards, etc., are in question, but also the compilation or the printing of it.[181] Such agitation and propaganda may take the form of verbal communication, in conversation, speeches or letters.[182] However, direct counter-revolutionary intent is required; sometimes, it is said, the establishment of it 'requires the paying of particular attention to the moral-political make-up of the accused'.[183] On occasion the courts have paid insufficient heed to this and their verdicts have had to be overruled, as in the 1940 case of a member of a ship's crew prosecuted for 'utterances connected with his personal, unsatisfactory material position'.[184] 'A personal diary with an anti-Soviet content' does not fall under the terms of the article;[185] nor do 'deliberately incorrect statements and opinions about the official activities and way of life of indivi-dual leaders'.[186] This is, none the less, one of the legal norms that are the most readily open to abuse, if only in that the phrase 'with the aim of . . . weakening' the Soviet régime lends itself, if circumstances require, to the widest possible interpre-tation. Moreover, the new definitions are based on a wider formulation than the preceding one: the previously required presence of a 'call for the overthrow, etc.' no longer figures in it, and the phrase about 'slanderous distortions' has been newly added. One authority states that this charge was 'justifiably applied' to certain persons hostile to the Socialist system who expressed approval of the mutiny in Hungary, praised the actions of the mutineers and called for the restoration of capi-talist ways in the USSR'.[187] It could apply to the mutilation of busts and portraits of leaders and slogans.[188] It was the charge applied in the most notorious Soviet trial since the war, that of the writers Sinyavsky and Daniel in February, 1966. After be-ing subjected to defamatory Press abuse,[189] they were tried behind what were in effect closed doors. The one-sided nature of the trial and the severity of the sentences (Sinyavsky was

* The original sanctions as published in December, 1958, were markedly milder: a person could not, for instance, have been sentenced to deprivation of liberty *and* banishment.

sentenced to seven years and Daniel five in a 'strict régime' corrective labour colony[190]) evoked considerable disquiet at home and abroad.

(f) War Propaganda[191]

Definition: War propaganda in whatever form.

Sanction: From three to eight years deprivation of freedom, with or without banishment of from two to five years.

This article, not to put too fine a point on it, is legalistic window-dressing. It derives from the law of March 12, 1951, 'On the Defence of Peace',[192] since when no prosecutions have ever been brought under it in the USSR (though cases are said to have been brought in other East European countries[193]). Indeed. it is hard to see what purpose any such prosecutions could serve that would be germane to criminal law as such. This conclusion is borne out by the authoritative statement that 'it has great international significance and is a visible demonstration of the peace-loving policy of the Soviet State'.[194] It is also said to be 'highly unlikely that any such crimes will be committed in the USSR'.[195] A legal textbook has taken pains to point out that 'of course, a call to strengthen the defence capability of the USSR cannot be viewed as war propaganda'.[196] The same source claims that 'agitation' for the ends covered by the article also constitutes a *corpus delicti*.[197] Elsewhere it is stated that even a call for war against capitalist States contravenes the article.[198]

(g) Organisation of Specially Dangerous Crimes[199]

Definitions:

Organisational activity directed towards committing specially dangerous State crimes;

Participation in an anti-Soviet organisation.

Sanction: In accordance with the provisions governing each of the State crimes listed above.

This article is closely linked with Article 17 of the Bases of USSR Criminal Legislation of December, 1958, defining the constituent forms of co-participation as executants, organisers, instigators and accessories. Organisers of the crimes in question are deemed those who recruit members, work out plans and direct the execution of a plan; and they are regarded as 'the most dangerous participants in counter-revolutionary organisations'. They accordingly are liable in respect of the totality of the actions committed by the given organisation,[200] whereas other participants are normally only held responsible for those acts in which they directly participated. However, as regards the second definition in this article, it has been said that the mere fact of participating in an anti-Soviet organisation already establishes guilt, even if no counter-revolutionary action has in fact been committed.[201] Commentaries on this article point out, somewhat superfluously, that an expression of desire to join such an organisation cannot be regarded as participation in it.[202]

(h) Crimes Against Another Workers' State [203]

Definition: Specially dangerous crimes committed against another workers' State.

Sanction: According to the sanctions provided for the relevant crimes as listed above.

This clause, formulated 'in the interests of the international solidarity of the workers', dates back to 1927. It applies to all the People's Democracies.[204] No known prosecutions have been brought under it in recent years.

OTHER STATE CRIMES

These include:

(a) Violation of National or Racial Equality [205]

Definitions:

Propaganda or agitation with the aim of arousing racial or national hatred or differences;

Direct or indirect restriction of rights, or establishment of direct or indirect privileges of citizens, on the basis of their racial or national appurtenance.

Sanction: From six months to three years deprivation of freedom, or banishment from two to five years (previous upper limit—two years).

This article also covers the dissemination, preparation or keeping of literature directed to the above aim.[206] If, however, there is any counter-revolutionary intent it becomes anti-Soviet propaganda and agitation (see earlier); on the other hand, if such acts are based on personal hostility they cannot be qualified under this heading. The achievement of consequential results is not a necessary attribute; the initiation of such action

[95]

is sufficient.[207] The concrete expression of the attributes of this crime varies from republic to republic.

(b) Divulgence of State Secrets[208]

Definition: the divulgence of information constituting a State secret by a person to whom this information was entrusted or became known through his work or employment, where attributes of treason or espionage are absent.

Sanction: From two to five years deprivation of freedom; (in the event of grave consequences ensuing) from five to eight years deprivation of freedom (previously from five to 10 years).

Such divulgence can take the form of action or inaction, and be by word of mouth or in writing. It includes, for example, permitting unauthorised access to documents, careless talk to relatives, leaving documents around. It may be deliberate (with either direct or indirect intent) or through carelessness.[209] It is not required that the act of divulgence should be accompanied by the factual access of anyone else to the secrets in question.[210]

(c) Banditry[211]

Definitions:

The organising of armed bands with the aim of attacking State or public institutions and enterprises, or individuals;

Participation in such bands and in the attacks committed by them.

Sanction: From three to 15 years deprivation of freedom with confiscation of property and with or without banishment of from two to five years, or the death penalty with confiscation of property.

The terms of reference of banditry are comprehensive; a band need consist of no more than two members; a band is armed if only one of its members is in possession of a weapon (daggers or knives qualify, and this has been extended in judicial practice to axes and other implements); it is a 'band', as distinct from a group, provided there is some element of continuing stability and prior agreement (though it is not necessary that the intention to commit more than one criminal act be present). Similarly, the acts of organising a band,[212] of belonging to a band, or of participating in raids organised by a band—all together or any one in isolation constitute a *corpus delicti*. The motive may be either one of gain or of hooliganism; counter-revolutionary intent entails its requalification. Apart from organisers, regular and chance participants, other categories, such as those who provide the band with weapons, with material information or with means of concealment, also incur criminal liability under this article.[213] Trials for banditry have included two cases in 1961 of attacks on local militia stations to the east of Moscow: in the first case four of the defendants were shot and five received prison sentences of 15 years each, and in the latter three were shot.[214] It was not reported in either case that there had been any loss of life to the militia.

(d) Mass Disorders[215]

Definitions:

> The organisation of mass disorders accompanied by pogroms, destruction, arson and similar actions;
> The direct commission of the above crimes by participants in mass disorders, or the exertion by them of armed resistance to the authorities.

Sanction: From two to 15 years deprivation of freedom.

Mass disorders were frequent during the early years of the Revolution when, as one source says, they occurred 'in connection with shortages of foodstuffs, with delays in the payment of wages' and were, it is said, instigated by 'class hostile elements'.[216]

The present December, 1958, ruling indicated above differs from its predecessor in that it omits mass disorders characterised by disobedience to or resistance (unarmed) to the authorities.

For the 'aggravated' form of mass disorder set out above, all organisers and direct participants will continue to be criminally responsible. Yet the category of 'other participants' appears now to have been excluded; this follows on the lines of judicial practice which had tended to give such persons a 'conditional' sentence or acquit them.[217] However, as against this, it should be noted that the phrase 'and similar actions' has been stated to cover 'the illegal release of a person under arrest'.[218]

Although a recent source indicated that this crime is now rare,[219] an addition to the RSFSR Criminal Code in 1965[220] (making a person previously convicted of the crime a 'particularly dangerous recidivist' on committing another specified crime) suggested that it is still causing concern.

(e) *Illegal Departure Abroad or Illegal Entry into the USSR*[221]

Definition: Departure across the frontier, or entry into the USSR, or frontier crossing without a passport or the permission of the appropriate authorities.

Sanction: From one to three years deprivation of freedom. (Not applicable to foreigners entering the USSR for the purpose of utilising the right of asylum.)

This article is in effect the counterpart of that section of the article on treason (Article 1) defining 'flight abroad': where there is no element of treason or counter-revolutionary intent, illegal departure is qualified under this heading. It is noteworthy that the December, 1958, formulation, like previous ones, makes no distinction between officials or private persons.

(There are also the following two offences which though still marked among State crimes in All-Union legislation are located under other headings in the RSFSR Criminal Code. They still belong, however, to all intents and purposes, to the category of State crimes.)

(f) *Failure to Report State Crimes*[222]

Definition: Failure to report at the time of their preparation or commission offences of treason, espionage, terrorism, wrecking, sabotage, organisation of especially dangerous crimes, banditry, counterfeiting. (The RSFSR Code extends it to the following crimes: murder; aggravated rape; aggravated robbery; aggravated theft; robbery of State property with violence (*razboi*); aggravated or large-scale theft of property; aggravated fraud (*moshennichestvo*); attacks on militiamen or *druzhinniki*).)[223]

Sanction: From one to three years deprivation of freedom, or corrective labour for from six months to one year.

The December, 1958, list of State crimes, failure to report the commission of any of the latter itself being a crime, exhibits only two advantages over the previous definitions: it no longer includes any criminal liability for failure to report on anti-Soviet agitation and propaganda or on mass disorders. Relatives or friends of the offender continue to bear the same liability as anyone else.[224] At the same time subsequent legislation has extended the purview of the 1958 list to take in a number of offences not formally classified as State crimes.

It is relevant that a 1958 textbook on Soviet Criminal Law declared:

'There may, however, be in our country individuals who still do not consider it their civic duty, their moral obligation, actively and in good time to assist the punitive organs to uncover and unmask all who prepare to commit or commit a counter-revolutionary crime.'[225]

(g) Concealment of a State Crime[226]

Definition: Concealment, not promised in advance, of the criminal, of the weapons or means for committing the crime, of the traces of the crime, or of criminally acquired articles.

Sanction: (in relation to 11 specified State crimes, out of a total of 25). From one to five years deprivation of freedom with or without banishment for from two to five years, or banishment for up to five years. (In relation to crimes specified under (f), together with aggravated speculation, bribery and aggravated driving offences) up to five years deprivation of freedom or corrective labour for up to one year.[227] (In relation to other, specified, minor offences) up to two years deprivation of freedom or corrective labour for up to one year.[228]

This formulation, though a wide one, of the scope of 'concealment', is an advance on the previous RSFSR Criminal Code which identified it with 'complicity' and thus made it punishable in respect of all crimes.[229]

The remaining crimes included under the heading of 'other State crimes' in the December, 1958, and subsequent enactments are:

(a) loss of documents containing State secrets: one to three years; or three to eight years;[230]

(b) smuggling: three to 10 years plus confiscation,[231] with or without two to five years banishment.

(c) refusal to obey call-up orders: one to three years, or one to five years;[232]

(d) refusal to obey mobilisation orders: three to 10 years or death penalty (in wartime);[233]

(e) refusal in wartime to obey labour conscription or pay taxes: one to five years, or six months to one year's corrective labour;[234]

(f) violation of regulations for international flights: one to 10 years, or fine of up to 10,000 roubles with or without confiscation of plane;[235]

(g) violation of transport regulations: three to 15 years; or one to three years; or up to one year's corrective labour;[236]

(h) damaging of transport or signal communications: three to 15 years with or without two to five years banishment;[237]

(i) counterfeiting of currency or notes: three to 15 years with confiscation of property, with or without two to five years banishment or (if on large scale) 10 to 15 years deprivation of freedom with confiscation of property, and with or without two to five years banishment, or death penalty with confiscation of property;[238]

(j) violation of currency regulations and currency speculation: three to eight years with confiscation of stock, with or without two to five years banishment; or (if on large scale) five to 15 years deprivation of freedom with confiscation of property and with or without banishment of two to five years, or death penalty with confiscation of property,[239]

(k) attacks by prisoners on personnel of prisons or colonies: eight to 15 years deprivation of freedom or death penalty.[240]

OTHER CRIMES

Criminal offences, other than the State crimes dealt with in the preceding section, were not covered by All-Union normative acts in December, 1958, but were the subject of subsequent republican legislation embodied in the derivative Republican Criminal Codes, which were drafted in retrospective conformity with the All-Union principles of 1958. Thus the RSFSR Criminal Code devotes the following sections to non-State crimes:

Section 2: crimes against Socialist property;

Section 3: crimes against the life, health, liberty and dignity of the individual;

Section 4: crimes against the political and work rights of citizens;

Section 5: crimes against the personal property of citizens;
Section 6: economic crimes;
Section 7: crimes by officials;
Section 8. crimes against justice;
Section 9: crimes against the administrative order *;
Section 10: crimes against public safety, public order and the health of the population;
Section 11: crimes representing survivals of local customs;
Section 12: military crimes.

What is particularly striking about this body of criminal law is not so much the detail it enters into but the range it covers. In the field of official crimes its extremely wide definitions concerning abuse of office, exceeding of powers, failure to take action, etc., extend severally or totally to all Soviet officials who by definition range from factory managers to shop assistants, from inspectors to ministerial employees, from managers of State Farms to procurement representatives. Similarly as regards the coverage in terms of day-to-day activities, criminal activity may be expressed in anything from a theft of apples from a collective orchard[242] to the private production of religious literature.[243]

SOURCES

1. Piontkovsky, *Ucheniye o Prestuplenii*, p. 23, and *Sovetskoye Gosudarstvo i Pravo*, No. 10, 1964, p. 94 (Shlyapochnikov).

2. Piontkovsky, *Ucheniye o Prestuplenii*, p. 97.

3. *Ibid.*, pp. 97–9, and Sakharov, p. 88.

4. *Sovetskoye Gosudarstvo i Pravo*, No. 1, 1967, p. 33 (Piontkovsky).

5. *Ibid.*, No. 5, 1964, pp. 148–9 (Symposium held by All-Union Institute for Studying the Causes of, and Working out Measures for the Prevention of Crime).

* This section is held to include the three important additions to Article 190 (which is, strictly speaking, in Section 8) of September, 1966, concerning (1) the regular dissemination of fabrications discrediting the Soviet system; (2) insults to the Soviet or any Union-Republican shield or flag; (3) the organisation of, or active participation in, group activities which violate public order, etc. The maximum penalty in the cases of (1) and (3) is three years and of (2) two years deprivation of freedom.[241]

6. *Sovetskoye Gosudarstvo i Pravo*, No. 10, 1964, pp. 97–9 (Shlyapochnikov).
7. *Sotsialisticheskaya Zakonnost*, No. 1, 1961, p. 47 (Smirnov).
8. Tkachenko, p. 10.
9. Leist, p. 34.
10. *Entsiklopedichesky Slovar Pravovykh Znanii*, p. 270. Also *ibid.*, p. 343.
11. *Tass* in English, April 13, 1966.
12. *Sotsialisticheskaya Zakonnost*, No. 1, 1967, pp. 25, 26–7 (Savitsky).
13. *Komsomolskaya Pravda*, May 25, 1966 (Shlyapochnikov).
14. *Kommunist*, No. 12, 1966, pp. 62–3; *Ugolovnoe Pravo, Chast Osobennaya*, p. 258n.
15. *Sovetskoye Gosudarstvo i Pravo*, No. 1, 1966, p. 103 (Boldyrev); *see also: Komsomolskaya Pravda*, October 7, 1966 (Nikiforov and Senatov).
16. e.g. *Byulleten Ispolnitelnogo Komiteta Moskovskogo Gorodskogo Soveta Deputatov Trudyashchikhsya*, No. 2, 1966.
17. e.g. *Ugolovnoe Pravo, Chast Osobennaya*, pp. 7–8.
18. e.g. *Sovetskoye Gosudarstvo i Pravo*, No. 3, 1957, pp. 48 and 50; *ibid.*, No. 11, 1965, p. 104; *Problemy Iskoreniya Prestupnosti*, p. 52.
19. December, 1958, Bases of Judicial Structure, art. 2.
20. December, 1958, Bases of Criminal Legislation, art. 1.
21. See *Sorok Let Sovetskogo Prava*, p. 508.
22. December, 1958, Bases of Criminal Legislation, art. 7.
23. *Sovetskoye Gosudarstvo i Pravo*, No. 11, 1959, p. 57 (Piontkovsky); and Piontkovsky, *Ucheniye o Prestuplenii*, pp. 328–33.
24. *Novoye Ugolovnoye Zakonodatelstvo RSFSR*, pp. 55–8.
25. Rivlin, p. 26.
26. Piontkovsky and Menshagin, p. 72.
27. *Sovetskoye Ugolovnoye Pravo—Osobennaya Chast*, p. 8.
28. *Sotsialisticheskaya Zakonnost*, No. 1, 1962, p. 27 (Stepichev).
29. Brainin, pp. 221–2 (re Utevsky).
30. Solovyev, pp. 91–2.
31. *Ibid.*, p. 93.
32. Kriger, p. 246.
33. *Ibid.*, pp. 246–7; Chermensky, p. 35.
34. Kriger, pp. 247–9; Chermensky, p. 35.
35. Solovyev, pp. 94–6; and December, 1958, Bases of Criminal Legislation, art. 32.
36. Karpets, p. 10; *see also* for discussion of divergent views, Brainin, pp. 149–160.
37. December, 1958, Bases of Criminal Legislation, art. 20; and RSFSR Criminal Code, art. 20.
38. Karpets, p. 41.
39. *Novoye Ugolovnoye Zakonodatelstvo RSFSR*, p. 182, and *see also Sovetskoye Gosudarstvo i Pravo*,

No. 1, 1964, pp. 93–103 (*re* corrective labour laws).

40. *Sovetskoye Gosudarstvo i Pravo*, No. 1, 1964, p. 94 (Remenson); and No. 5, 1964, p. 71 (Struchkov).
41. See *Sorok Let Sovetskogo Prava*, pp. 550–1.
42. *Ibid.*, p. 553.
43. *Problemy Iskoreniya Prestupnosti*, p. 49.
44. Leist, p. 37.
45. *Izvestiya*, February 12, 1957 (speech by Rumyantsev).
46. Leist, p. 38.
47. *Komsomolskaya Pravda*, October 7, 1966 (Perlov warned against the retributive view; Nikoforov stressed the existence of the element of chastisement).
48. Feifer, pp. 68–9.
49. Gorshenin, p. 38.
50. December, 1958, Bases of Criminal Legislation, art. 21.
51. RSFSR Criminal Code, art. 21.
52. *Ibid.*, art. 22.
53. RSFSR *Laws*, 1917, 1 (Decree of the All-Russian Congress of Soviets of October 26, 1917).
54. *Pravda*, February 10, 1918.
55. RSFSR *Laws*, 1918, 44 (Decree of the RSFSR People's Commissariat of Justice of June 16, 1918).
56. RSFSR *Laws*, 1920, 4–5: 22 (Decree of the All-Russian Central Executive Committee and the Council of People's Commissars of January 17, 1920).
57. RSFSR *Laws*, 1920, 54: 236 (Article 1 of the Decree 'On the Bringing into Operation of the "Regulations Concerning Military Revolutionary Tribunals" ').
58. *Vedomosti Verkhovnogo Soveta SSSR*, No. 17, 1947 (Edict of the Presidium of the USSR Supreme Soviet of May 26, 1947).
59. *Vedomosti Verkhovnogo Soveta SSSR*, No. 3, 1950 (Edict of the Presidium of the USSR Supreme Soviet of January 12, 1950). According to *Osobo-Opasnye Gosudarstvennye Prestupleniya*, p. 64—'the national Republics, trade unions, peasants' organisations and also cultural figures' petitioned the USSR Supreme Soviet to this effect.
60. *Vedomosti Verkhovnogo Soveta SSSR*, No. 11, 1954 (Edict of the Presidium of the USSR Supreme Soviet of April 30, 1954).
61. (respectively) *Vedomosti Verkhovnogo Soveta SSSR*, No. 19, 1961 (Edict of the Presidium of the USSR Supreme Soviet of May 5, 1961); No. 27, 1961 (Edict of July 1, 1961); No. 8, 1962 (Edict of February 15, 1962—item 83); No. 8, 1962 (Edict of February 15, 1962—item 84); and No. 8, 1962 (Edict of February 15, 1962—item 85).
62. RSFSR Criminal Code, art. 23.

63. *Sovetskoye Gosudarstvo i Pravo*, No. 5, 1966, p. 70 (Zagorodnikov).
64. RSFSR *Laws*, 1922, 51: 646.
65. Savitsky and Rozenbaum, p. 14, and *Sovetskoye Gosudarstvo i Pravo*, No. 1, 1964, p. 105 (Natashev).
66. RSFSR *Laws*, 1923, 8: 108.
67. USSR *Laws*, 1930, 26: 344.
68. December, 1958, Bases of Criminal Legislation, art. 24, and RSFSR Criminal Code, arts. 25–6.
69. *Byulleten Verkhovnogo Suda SSSR*, No. 4, 1962, p. 14.
70. *Ispravitelno-Trudovoe Pravo*, pp. 149–50, 238–9.
71. *Byulleten Verkhovnogo Suda SSSR*, No. 4, 1962, art. 23, and RSFSR art. 24.
72. *Ibid.*, art. 23, and RSFSR art. 24.
73. *Ibid.*, art. 23, and RSFSR art. 24.
74. *Ibid.*, art. 38.
75. *Ibid.*, art. 44.
76. RSFSR art. 53.
77. *Entsiklopedichesky Slovar Pravovykh Znanii*, pp. 486–7.
78. *Sotsialisticheskaya Zakonnost*, No. 1, 1959, p. 179 (Speech by Rudenko).
79. *Sorok Let Sovetskogo Prava*, p. 491.
80. Belyaev, p. 11.
81. RSFSR *Laws*, 1922, 15:32 (Article 35 of RSFSR Criminal Code).
82. December, 1958, Bases of Criminal Legislation, art. 25, and RSFSR Criminal Code, art. 27.
83. *Ibid.*, art. 25.
84. *Vedomosti Verkhovnogo Soveta SSSR*, No. 13, 1961 (Edict of the Presidium of the Supreme Soviet of the USSR of March 25, 1961).
85. RSFSR Criminal Code, Appendix (arts. 1–6).
86. December, 1958, Bases of Criminal Legislation, art. 10, and RSFSR Criminal Code, art. 10.
87. *Sovetskoye Gosudarstvo i Pravo*, No. 4, 1965, p. 65 (Karpushin).
88. USSR *Laws*, 1935, 19.
89. *Vedomosti Verkhovnogo Soveta*, No. 25, 1941 (Edict of the Presidium of the USSR Supreme Soviet of May 31, 1941).
90. RSFSR *Laws*, 1918, 16: 227; and 1920, 13:83.
91. RSFSR Criminal Code, art. 23.
92. December, 1958, Bases of Criminal Legislation, art. 23, and RSFSR Criminal Code, art. 24.
93. *Ibid.*, art. 24, and RSFSR arts. 25 and 26.
94. *Vestnik Moskovskogo Universiteta*, No. 1, 1965, p. 35 (Spiridonov); *Sovetskoye Gosudarstvo i Pravo*, No. 2, 1965, p. 20 (Pankratov).
95. *Pravda*, March 3, 1966.
96. RSFSR *Laws*, 1917, 4.
97. RSFSR *Laws*, 1919, 66: 590.
98. RSFSR *Laws*, 1922, 1.
99. RSFSR *Laws*, 1922, 15: 32.
100. USSR *Laws*, 1924, 24:13.

101. USSR *Laws,* 1929, 76: 732.
102. USSR *Laws,* 1932, 62: 360.
103. *Sorok Let Sovetskogo Prava,* p. 504.
104. Shargorodsky, pp. 179–80.
105. December, 1958, Law on the Abolition of Deprivation of Electoral Rights.
106. RSFSR Criminal Code, art. 57.
107. *Ibid.*
108. *Entsiklopedichesky Slovar Pravovykh Znanii,* p. 453.
109. *Sorok Let Sovetskogo Prava,* p. 486.
110. *Ibid.,* p. 486.
111. *Ibid.,* p. 487.
112. *Ibid.,* p. 485 and p. 504.
113. USSR *Laws,* 1934, 64: 459.
114. USSR *Laws,* 1937, 61: 266.
115. *Sorok Let Sovetskogo Prava,* p. 486.
116. *Sbornik Deistvuyushchikh Postanovlenii Plenuma Verkhovnogo Suda SSSR,* p. 5.
117. *Sorok Let Sovetskogo Prava,* p. 487 and p. 489.
118. *Osobo-Opasnye Gosudarstvennye Prestupleniya,* pp. 26–30.
119. *Sovetskoye Gosudarstvo i Pravo,* No. 5, 1964 pp. 79–87 (Anashkin).
120. *Osobo-Opasnye Gosudarstvennye Prestupleniya,* pp. 13–14.
121. December, 1958, Law on Criminal Liability for State Crimes, art. 1, and RSFSR Criminal Code, art. 64.
122. RSFSR Criminal Code, art. 64, as amended by Edict of Presidium of Supreme Soviet of July 15, 1962 (*Sovetskaya Yustitsiya,* Nos. 15–16, 1962, p. 30).
123. USSR *Laws,* 1929, 76: 732.
124. USSR *Laws,* 1934, 30: 173.
125. *Ibid.*
126. Piontkovsky and Menshagin, p. 147.
127. *Sovetskoye Ugolovnoye Pravo—Osobennaya Chast,* p. 38.
128. Piontkovsky and Menshagin, p. 146.
129. Turetsky, p. 40.
130. USSR *Laws,* 1934, 30: 173. See *Osobo-Opasnye Gosudarstvennye Prestupleniya,* p. 75.
131. Piontkovsky and Menshagin, p. 155.
132. *Voprosy Kodifikatsii Sovetskogo Prava,* p. 92.
133. *Sovetskoye Ugolovnoye Pravo—Osobennaya Chast,* p. 38.
134. December, 1958, Bases of Criminal Legislation, art. 17, and RSFSR Criminal Code, art. 17.
135. *Sovetskoye Ugolovnoye Pravo—Osobennaya Chast,* p. 40.
136. *Osobo-Opasnye Gosudarstvennye Prestupleniya,* p. 86.
137. *Ugolovnoye Pravo, Chast Osobennaya,* p. 30 and footnote.
138. Revised (1956) List of State Secrets given in *Sovetskoye Ugolovnoye Pravo—Osobennaya Chast,* pp. 35–6.
139. *Ibid.,* p. 37.

140. *Osobo-Opasnye Gosudarstvennye Prestupleniya*, pp. 97–8.
141. Turetsky, p. 44n.
142. *Vedomosti Verkhovnogo Soveta SSSR*, No. 3, 1960 (Edict of the Presidium of the USSR Supreme Soviet of January 13, 1960).
143. *Izvestiya-Nedelya*, No. 35, 1962.
144. December, 1958, Law on Criminal Liability for State Crimes, art. 2, and RSFSR Criminal Code, art. 65.
145. *Osobo-Opasnye Gosudarstvennye Prestupleniya*, p. 90.
146. *Ugolovnoye Pravo, Chast Osobennaya*, p. 34n.
147. December, 1958, Law on Criminal Liability for State Crimes, art. 3, and (RSFSR) art. 66.
148. RSFSR *Laws*, 1922, 15: 153 (Article 64[3] of RSFSR Criminal Code).
149. Piontkovsky and Menshagin, pp. 172–3.
150. *Sovetskoye Ugolovnoye Pravo—Osobennaya Chast*, p. 46; Turetsky, pp. 59–60.
151. Turetsky, p. 60.
152. *Ibid.*
153. *Osobo-Opasnye Gosudarstvennye Prestupleniya*, p. 107.
154. *Ibid.*, p. 110.
155. *Ugolovnoe Pravo, Chast Osobennaya*, p. 41.
156. *Sovetskoye Ugolovnoye Pravo—Osobennaya Chast*, p. 46.
157. December, 1958, Law on Criminal Liability for State Crimes, art. 4, and RSFSR Criminal Code, art. 69.

158. *Ibid.*, art. 5, and (RSFSR) art. 68.
159. Piontkovsky and Menshagin, p. 187.
160. *Sovetskoye Ugolovnoye Pravo—Osobennaya Chast*, p. 50.
161. *Osobo-Opasnye Gosudarstvennye Prestupleniya*, pp. 134–5.
162. *Oktyabr*, No. 3, 1966, p. 213.
163. *Osobo-Opasnye Gosudarstvennye Prestupleniya*, p. 39.
164. *Sovetskoe Ugolovnoye Pravo—Osobennaya Chast*, p. 51.
165. Piontkovsky and Menshagin, p. 188.
166. *Ibid.*, p. 188.
167. December, 1958, Law on Criminal Liability for State Crimes, art. 6, and RSFSR Criminal Code, art. 69.
168. *Sovetskoye Ugolovnoye Pravo—Osobennaya Chast*, p. 52.
169. *Ibid.*, p. 52.
170. *Osobo-Opasnye Gosudarstvennye Prestupleniya*, p. 145.
171. *Ibid.*, p. 148.
172. RSFSR *Laws*, 1922, 15 (Article 63 of RSFSR Criminal Code).
173. RSFSR *Laws*, 1923, 48: 480 (Decree of All-Russian Central Executive Committee of July 10, 1923).
174. Turetsky, pp. 68–9.
175. *Ugolovnoye Pravo, Chast Osobennaya*, p. 49.
176. *Sovetskoye Ugolovnoye Pravo—Osobennaya Chast*, p. 51.
177. *Ibid.*, p. 51.

178. *Osobo-Opasnye Gosudarstvennye Prestupleniya*, p. 155.
179. *Ibid.*, p. 149.
180. December, 1958, Law on Criminal Responsibility for State Crimes, art. 7, and RSFSR Criminal Code, art. 70.
181. Piontkovsky and Menshagin, p. 196.
182. *Sovetskoye Ugolovnoye Pravo*, p. 54.
183. Piontkovsky and Menshagin, p. 195.
184. *Ibid.*, p. 195.
185. Turetsky, p. 77.
186. *Ugolovnoye Pravo, Osobennaya Chast*, p. 45.
187. *Osobo-Opasnye Gosudarstvennye Prestupleniya*, p. 126.
188. *Ibid.*, p. 127.
189. *Literaturnaya Gazeta*, January 22, 1966 (Kedrina —one of the 'communal prosecutors' at the trial itself); *Izvestiya*, January 13, 1966 (Eremin).
190. *Pravda*, February 15, 1966.
191. December, 1958, Law on Criminal Responsibility for State Crimes, art. 8, and RSFSR Criminal Code, art. 70.
192. *Vedomosti Verkhovnogo Soveta*, No. 5, 1951.
193. *Osobo-Opasnye Gosudarstvennye Prestupleniya*, pp. 172–3.
194. *Sovetskoye Gosudarstvo i Pravo*, No. 2, 1960, p. 24 (Romashkin).
195. *Osobo-Opasnye Gosudarstvennye Prestupleniya*, p. 174, and also *Novoye Ugolovnoye Zakonodatelstvo RSFSR*, p. 48.
196. *Ugolovnoye Pravo, Chast Osobennaya*, p. 39.
197. *Ibid.*, p. 38.
198. Turetsky, p. 81.
199. December, 1958, Law on Criminal Responsibility for State Crimes, art. 9, and RSFSR Criminal Code, art. 72.
200. Piontkovsky and Menshagin, p. 201.
201. *Osobo-Opasnye Gosudarstvennye Prestupleniya*, p. 205.
202. *Ugolovnoye Pravo, Chast Osobennaya*, p. 55; Turetsky, p. 87.
203. December, 1958, Law on Criminal Responsibility for State Crimes, art. 10, and RSFSR Criminal Code, art. 73.
204. Piontkovsky and Menshagin, p. 136.
205. December, 1958, Law on Criminal Responsibility for State Crimes, art. 11, and RSFSR Criminal Code, art. 74.
206. Piontkovsky and Menshagin, p. 242.
207. *Ibid.*, p. 242.
208. December, 1958, Law on Criminal Responsibility for State Crimes, art. 12, and RSFSR Criminal Code, art. 75.
209. Kirichenko, p. 174.
210. *Sovetskoye Ugolovnoye Pravo—Osobennaya Chast*, pp. 372–3; *Ugolovnoye Pravo, Chast Osobennaya*, p. 68n.
211. December, 1958, Law on Criminal Responsibility for State Crimes, art. 14, and

RSFSR Criminal Code, art. 77.

212. Piontkovsky, *Ucheniye o Prestuplenii*, p. 566.

213. *See* Piontkovsky and Menshagin, pp. 223–38.

214. *Vechernaya Moskva*, August 17, 1961 (re Murom); *Tass*, September 5, 1961 (re Vladimir).

215. December, 1958, Law on Criminal Responsibility for State Crimes, art. 16, and RSFSR Criminal Code, art. 79.

216. Piontkovsky and Menshagin, pp. 246–7.

217. *Sovetskoye Ugolovnoye Pravo—Osobennaya Chast*, p. 66; *Ugolovnoe Pravo, Chast Osobennaya*, p. 91.

218. Piontkovsky and Menshagin, p. 250.

219. *Ugolovnoye Pravo, Chast Osobennaya*, p. 91.

220. *Vedomosti Verkhovnogo Soveta RSFSR*, No. 27, 1965, p. 523.

221. December, 1958, Law on Criminal Responsibility for State Crimes, art. 20, and RSFSR Criminal Code, art. 84.

222. *Ibid.*, art. 26; and RSFSR Criminal Code, art. 190 and art. 88[1], as formulated in *Sovetskaya Yustitsiya*, Nos. 15–16, 1962, p. 29.

223. RSFSR Criminal Code, art. 190, as amended by an Edict of the RSFSR Supreme Soviet of July 25, 1962 (*Sovetskaya Yustitsiya*, Nos. 15–16, 1962, p. 28).

224. Piontkovsky and Menshagin, p. 203.

225. *Sovetskoye Ugolovnoye Pravo—Osobennaya Chast*, p. 57.

226. *Sovetskaya Yustitsiya*, No. 6, 1961, p. 6 (Edict of Supreme Soviet of February 24, 1961) and RSFSR Criminal Code, art. 88[2], as formulated in *Sovetskaya Yustitsiya*, Nos. 15–16, 1962, p. 29.

227. RSFSR Criminal Code, art. 189, as amended by Edict of RSFSR Supreme Court of July 25, 1962 (*Sovetskaya Yustitsiya*, Nos. 15–16, 1962, p. 28).

228. *Ibid.*

229. *Novoye Ugolovnoye Zakonodatelstvo RSFSR*, p. 58.

230. December, 1958, Law on Criminal Responsibility for State Crimes, art. 13, and RSFSR Criminal Code, art. 76.

231. *Ibid.* (December, 1958), art. 15, and (RSFSR) art. 78, as amended by Edict of the RSFSR Supreme Soviet of July 25, 1962 (*Sovetskaya Yustitsiya*, Nos. 15–16, 1962, p. 28).

232. *Ibid.* (December, 1958), art. 17, and (RSFSR) art. 80.

233. *Ibid.* (December, 1958), art. 18, and (RSFSR) art. 81.

234. *Ibid.* (December, 1958), art. 19, and (RSFSR) art. 82.

235. *Ibid.* (December, 1958), art. 21, and (RSFSR) art. 84.

236. *Ibid.* (December, 1958), art. 22, and (RSFSR) art. 85.

237. *Ibid.* (December, 1958), art. 23, and (RSFSR) art. 86, as amended by Edict of the RSFSR Supreme Soviet of July 25, 1962 (*Sovetskaya Yustitsiya,* Nos. 15–16, 1962, p. 30).
238. *Ibid.* (December, 1958), art. 24, and (RSFSR) art. 87 (*Sovetskaya Yustitsiya,* p. 27).
239. *Ibid.* (December, 1958), art. 25, and (RSFSR) art. 88 (*Sovetskaya Yustitsiya,* p. 27).
240. RSFSR Criminal Code, art. 77^2, as amended by Edict of July 25, 1962 (*Sovetskaya Yustitsiya,* Nos. 15–16, 1962, p. 29).
241. *Vedomosti Verkhovnogo Soveta RSFSR,* No. 38, 1966, p. 819.
242. Solovyev, p. 173.
243. *Moskovskaya Pravda,* August 13, 1965.

V

Party Control and Socialist Legality

The ultimate force behind the organs of justice is the Communist Party and the ultimate rationale behind the direction taken by Soviet law has tended to be its relationship to Party policy.

'In the activity of the organs of investigation, of the Prosecutor's Office and of the courts, as of all organs of the Soviet State, the directing and guiding rôle belongs to the Communist Party of the Soviet Union. While obeying the law in all their activity and securing its unwavering observance by all officials and citizens, the organs of investigation, the Prosecutor's Office and the courts carry out the policy of the Communist Party expressed in law.'[1]

This theme continued to be constant after Stalin's death. The courts, it is said:

'cannot carry out any other policy than the policy of the Communist Party and the Soviet government'.[2]

or,

'The prosecutor, however, cannot consistently carry into effect the principle of independence if he is not connected with the Party organs ... Soviet prosecutors are guided in their work by the directives of the Party Congresses and of the Central Committee of the CPSU, by the directives of Party organs in the Union Republics and in the localities.'[3]

or,

'The prosecutor's office is guided in its activity by the directing instructions of the Central Committee of our Party which determine the basis of our State and political life.'[4]

More recently the Chairman of the RSFSR Supreme Court took Soviet courts to task for underestimating the rôle of communal institutions 'despite the direct directives of the Party'.[5] A textbook on the USSR Supreme Court has stated:

'The organisation of the judicial system, the political nature of and the direction taken by the activity of the courts, depend on in whose hands State power is located.'[6]

Thus Party directives can either bear directly on the framing of criminal liability, as did the decree of the Party Central Committee and the USSR Council of Ministers of May, 1939,[7] on measures to protect collective farm land, or take the form of general pronouncements 'from which practical inferences for the workers of the courts and the Prosecutor's Office inescapably follow'.[8] Laws are an expression of policy and it is essentially Party policy that, for instance, defines the area of anti-State crimes as well as the relative severity of the enforcement of laws governing any branch of activity. While what had been called 'the latitude for the application of a political criterion'[9] has been considerably restricted; this too was because of the Party changing its attitude.

Though, as has been noted, an important catalyst in this process has been the liberalising influence of the bulk of Soviet legal opinion, and to a lesser extent, the opportunities given to public opinion since Stalin's death to make itself heard, there is no formal, let alone practical, safeguard to prevent the Party authorities from retracting such concessions as they have made. What was said in 1950, before any modification had taken place, that 'the court is, in reality, a conductor of the policy of the Communist Party and the Soviet régime'[10] remains axiomatic, though the room for manœuvre afforded by this axiom can vary a great deal in practice and in time.

Just as the Communist Party retains control over all 'commanding heights', so too in terms of membership alone, its control over the judicial organs is striking. No figures of Party membership of prosecutors, where it may be presumed to be at its highest, are available; it is known that the opinion of local Party organisations is sought in making out testimonial certificates about prosecutors.[11] Such limited figures as have been published are noteworthy, however. In 1964, 3,120 of the 3,413 people's judges elected in the RSFSR were Party members or candidate members; in 1966, the 'overwhelming majority' of all people's judges were said to be Communists.[12] About 44 per cent of all people's assessors were stated in 1965 to be Party or candidate members.[13] As of 1960 53 per cent of all the RSFSR defence lawyers were members or candidate members of the Party.[14]

Very little data are revealed about the actual executive control over, or interference in the work of the judiciary exerted by Party organs but there can be no doubt that, whatever the formal terms of reference of the judiciary, these two factors are of great practical importance. Some sidelight was thrown on this relationship in connection with an investigation by the Ukrainian Ministry of Justice into large-scale thefts in the Vinnitsa region in 1953;[15] the *oblast* court, the local prosecutors and the defence lawyers involved had, it was said, all been to blame for the acquittal of the criminals when brought to trial. The inspector sent to the spot by the Ministry was rebuked for not 'resorting to the aid of local Party organisations' in his examination of the case, while the local Party Committee was attacked for not taking 'every step for a complete purge of the *oblast* court, the prosecutor's office and the collegium of defence lawyers of all that was worthless'.

This case demonstrated that Party organs wielded what amounted to powers of dismissal in relation to all organs of the judiciary, prosecutors and defence lawyers included. Even today, the corollary of Party expulsion would probably be dismissal.

In the above case, it was the Party authorities who were responsible for the dismissals, thus usurping the powers of those organs formally empowered to effect them. It is theoretically the case that judges cannot be disciplined in the event of the subsequent alteration of their sentences by a higher instance, provided that these sentences are in accordance with the law and their own inner convictions:[16] that there is a need still to spell this out speaks for itself. (In fact, there was a complaint in 1965 that defence lawyers are sometimes liable to disciplining if their clients are convicted.[17])

The right in practice of Party organs to dismiss members of the judiciary from their posts, though nowhere to be found in any legislative enactment, was also signalised by a 1957 ruling of the Omsk regional Party Committee,[18] the Bureau of which recorded that the Deputy Chairman of the Omsk regional court

'deserved to be dismissed from his post and expelled from the Party, but it took into account that he had recognised the error of his action and had no previous penalties, and administered him a reprimand to be recorded in his Party card'.

Glimpses of the part played behind the scenes by local Party organisations are revealed from time to time when particularly bad miscarriages of justice are exposed. In a case in which

Gaskov, a critical journalist in the town of Armavir, was unjustly imprisoned:

'One cannot reproach the heads of the Armavir town Party Committee with ignorance and indifference. On the contrary, they devoted exceptional attention to the Gaskov case. The Bureau of the town Committee passed resolutions on the case three times; not counting the numerous instances of interference with the course of the investigation . . .

'For example, in the Bureau's . . . resolution of December 21, 1963, it was stated that the town prosecutor . . . "displayed laggardliness and indecision" although "all grounds for bringing Gaskov to criminal responsibility existed".'[19]

The reaction of higher Party authorities to the case was also revealing: a superior of the prosecutor involved was blamed, among others things, for not keeping the Party organs (i.e. presumably the 'administrative organs' responsible for police and judicial matters) informed, and the Party Secretary chiefly concerned was condemned for his 'incompetent interference'.[20]

It was the manner of the interference, rather than the fact that it occurred, which aroused criticism.

Party organs are in a position to exert influence not only when they are acting on orders received but also when they are doing so for other motives. Such evidence as exists shows that the interests of Party organisations or even the fact of Party membership tend to influence the course of justice. In one case[21] of the trial of a Party member before a local People's Court, the Secretary of the Semipalatinsk Party Committee 'took him under his protection and began to seek his acquittal'. Elsewhere the dismissal from his job of a Tadzhik criminal investigator who had unwisely brought a relative of the local *raikom* first secretary to book for an offence of group rape was only reversed on the intervention of the Tadzhik Central Committee: in this context the *raikom* secretary had told the overzealous investigator that 'The law is the law, but the secretary of the *raikom* is the secretary of the *raikom*.'[22] In a similar (1962) case concerning the failure to institute criminal proceedings against a Party member due to the protection of the local Party authorities, the Vyazma town Committee Party secretary pronounced that 'it is the Party organ which decides whether a Communist is to be tried or not tried in court'.[23] References to, and warnings against, such practices continue to be pub-

lished.[24] The publicising of such instances of unjustified intercession by Party organs in the judicial trial of a Party member
tends to indicate not only that such interference with the course
of justice does take place but that it will often attain its aim
unless checked as a result of forceful and high-level intervention by the Party authorities themselves.

The Soviet judiciary, be it judges, prosecutors or investigators, is not always as unresponsive as it should be to social
pressure. A 1962 article in a Soviet legal journal stated:

'It must be confessed that numerous feuilletons in our Press
dealing with lack of principle on the part of prosecutors or judges
when they come up against the children of "VIPs" are well
founded . . . To some degree all these items testify to the un-
principled position of jurists. And not only of jurists, unfortunately.
Court cases, as is well known, come up before other people besides
the judge. The people's assessors whom the workers elect from
among the most respected, most authoritative citizens, have an
equal say with that of the judge . . .'[25]

The judiciary is inextricably interwoven with the Party, even
within the court itself. An article in 1965 explained how the
Party cell of a People's Court achieved a 'considerably severer'
sentencing policy among judges who had failed to comprehend
certain provisions of the Party Programme.[26] Soviet sources
demonstrate the effect on the judiciary of Party-inspired 'cam-
paigns' either when things go badly awry or, more typically,
when judges are praised for their part in the 'struggle' against
a particular crime or category of crimes on which attention is
focused at the given time.[27] There appears to be a bias, at the
moment at least, towards severity of punishment. An analysis
of 842 cases, carried out in 1965–66, revealed that 32 per cent
of the judicial errors involved were caused by the inappro-
priateness of the sentences, either as regards the crime or the
personality of the defendant. In turn, nearly 80 per cent of the
errors in this category were due to excessive severity.[28]

The primacy of Party control often works in a reverse direction to what is currently termed 'Socialist legality'. As has been
ex post facto admitted of the early 1930s: 'in the conditions of
the drive against the *kulaks,* infringement of revolutionary
legality became a not infrequent phenomenon'.[29] In the late
1930s the employment by Party authorities of the extra-
judicial machinery of the NKVD Special Board 'infringed in
practice the principle of the uniformity and exclusive character

of judicial authority proclaimed for the organs of Socialist justice'.[30]

Now that Party policy is able to pursue a somewhat smoother course, many of the more immediately apparent contradictions between it and Socialist legality have, as it were, reconciled themselves (although continued warnings by lawyers about the impermissibility of any form of outside pressure on the courts suggest that such pressure still exists[31]). At the same time a different rift has been opening up elsewhere in the institutional field. While the extra-legal procedures and institutions of the inter-war years were abolished in the immediate post-Stalin period, a new retreat from legal guarantees was ushered in after the XX Congress which took the form of institutionalising communal forms of justice complementary to and at times in competition with the judicial system. As has already been noted, this derives from the hypotheses that crime is on the wane with the advance of Communism; that the vast majority of offenders are re-educable; and that conversely the unregenerate few now desire not less, but more severe punishment. These new (or renovated) institutions include:

(a) comrades' courts;
(b) collective probation;
(c) public ancillaries to the militia, the prosecutors and the judiciary, housing committees, etc.;
(d) special laws, e.g. on parasites.

The scope of, for want of a better word, communal justice in the Soviet Union is vast. It does not operate at the rarefied level of crimes like espionage or banditry, nor can it operate in schools,[32] but otherwise it is virtually all-pervasive: it both infiltrates the courts and also provides alternative tribunals. In place of procedural guarantees and professional justice, it offers the notion of civic justice and public morality. It is the subject of a persistent conflict between the proceduralists and the pragmatists. It has, for example, been said on the latter's behalf:

'There exists the view that the practice of settling criminal cases by public action tends towards widening the scope of criminal law. In this connection it was proposed to supplement the Criminal Code with a section setting out the norms which regulate in detail the settlement of criminal cases by public procedure. It was, for example, proposed that the comrades' courts should be converted into special first instance courts with their verdicts being subject to cassation appeal to the People's Court. Here we are dealing with an attempt to expand the sphere of law at the expense of the relations regulating norms of moral conduct. At the base of this attempt lies the conviction that the including of public forms of applying influence to offenders within the field of law will impart to these norms those features of stability that characterise jurisdiction and with which the high authority and immutability of legal decisions are usually associated and confer greater guarantees of the rights of the individual.'[33]

COMRADES' COURTS

The status, scope and functions of comrades' courts were regularised in mid-1961 under a regulatory order adopted by all the constituent republics.[34] This provided *inter alia* that:

Comrades' courts could be set up at factories, offices, organisations, higher educational establishments, collective farms, housing collectives, street committees where there was a collective to elect them of not less than 50 people. Their members, who co-opt their own chairman, are re-elected annually. They are responsible to the given collective and come under the direction of the appropriate TU Committee, or, in the case of collective farms, housing collectives and street committees, under that of the Executive Committee of the local Soviet.

The cases which they are entitled to hear include:
(1) infringements of labour discipline;
(2) drunkenness or disorderly behaviour in public or at work;
(3) unworthy conduct towards wife, children or parents;
(4) disturbances in flats and hostels; quarrels among inmates;
(5) property suits up to 50 roubles;
(6) 'other anti-social behaviour not involving criminal liability'; and
(7) minor offences referred to them by the militia, the prosecutor or the court.

They initiate hearings on the basis of applications from trade union committees, the *druzhinniks*, street committees and 'other public organisations or meetings of citizens', from the local Soviet and even 'on the basis of statements by citizens and on the initiative of the comrades' court itself'. They hold their sessions at the offender's place of work or employment out of working hours. Sessions are public, presided over by three members of the court with whose permission anyone present may comment or ask questions. A handbook states:

'One must bear in mind that even the most inveterate offender can be "taken down a peg or two" with the aid of questions and made to ponder his behaviour with the proper seriousness.'[35]

A record is kept. If the offender fails to put in an appearance, the case is referred back to the militia or the court; if he fails to appear for a second time without good reason, the case can be tried in his absence. Verdict is by majority of the members of the court.

The comrades' courts can impose the following:

(a) public apology;
(b) comradely caution;
(c) public condemnation;
(d) public reprimand with or without publication;
(e) fine of up to 10 roubles;*
(f) raise with the management, etc., the question of disciplinary action, e.g. transfer to lower-paid work.
(g) raise the question of eviction from accommodation;
(h) damages of up to 50 roubles in conjunction with any of the preceding sanctions.

If the accused genuinely repents, the court need take no action beyond the public hearing. If the court deems it necessary, it can refer the case back for trial. The resolution of the court is final, and where unjustified or illegal, can only be reviewed by the same court. The existing procedure which 'not infrequently gives rise to muddle in practice' has been criticised[36] and suggestions that the procuracy should be able to intervene in cases of illegal decisions have been made.[37]

Since the above provisions of mid-1961, the competence of the comrades' courts in the RSFSR has been substantially extended by a further edict of October 23, 1963, to cover, *inter alia*

(a) petty hooliganism, petty speculation, petty embezzlement of State property, petty theft (as first time offences);
(b) various property suits;

* The sum may be higher in specified cases by the terms of a 1965 amendment (*see* below).

[117]

(c) minor assault;

(d) 'other criminal actions not involving great social danger';

and, at the same time, their tenure of office has been increased from one to two years and they may be set up at places with a collective of under 25 people.[38] In January, 1965, there was a further extension of the rights of RSFSR comrades' courts. In cases of petty embezzlement of State or public property, they could levy fines of up to 30 roubles for a first offence and 50 for a second. The guilty party was also obliged to repay the material loss in full. Persons who had appeared before a comrades' court twice for petty embezzlement could not be tried by such a court again.[39]

While the comrades' courts are undoubtedly trespassing increasingly on the province of the regular courts, their strong point is officially deemed to be the fact that they can deal with actionable offences without being bound by standard judicial procedure.[40] It has been emphasised that they should be wary of copying standard legal terminology or norms:[41] they do not, it is said, have to prove the offender's 'guilt'.[42] It is the social-educational aspect that must prevail over the judicial one. Indeed it might at times be thought that the comrades' courts are primarily meant to contribute to the edification of the spectators:

'The educational influence of the comrades' courts is enhanced when the maximum number of members of the given collective attend at its sessions.'[43]

A handbook states that the main aim of the resolutions passed by these courts is their educational effect on the offender and the spectators.[44] There is no provision for defence counsel in any form but the underlying assumption is that the offender will confess his guilt. A jurist has proposed that only those offenders who admit their guilt should be handed over for extra-judicial measures; although this might prove something of a safeguard, he had himself previously stated that people sometimes plead guilty to crimes they have not committed. He also strongly criticised the imprecise wording of the regulations covering the handing over of cases for 'public' action.[45]

Needless to say the *carte blanche* given to comrades' courts does provide openings for victimisation, witting and unwitting. The amateur judges have themselves been known to exceed their powers and to fail to keep records of the proceedings.[46] It would appear that they are frequently rude and overbearing and seek to prevent those who wish to speak out in defence of the offender from doing so;[47] tact and delicacy are not always their strong point.[48] Perhaps the gravest objection to them is that there is hardly any suggestion that these revivalist-type tribunals can err in their findings. Nevertheless there are signs that the trade unions[49] (which they supersede in certain respects) had and still have reservations about them, as do several Soviet lawyers.[50] Either way, they are undoubtedly a power in the land; in 1965, there were said to be more than 220,000 comrades' courts in the country;[51] there were more than 153,000 in the RSFSR in 1967.[52]

COLLECTIVE PROBATION

The origins of collective probation (*peredacha na poruki*) are traced back to 1918.[53] But the effective adoption of it dates from the December, 1958, Bases and the subsequent Republican Codes of Criminal Procedure adopted in 1960–62. It has also been the subject of numerous decrees of the USSR Supreme Court. It is, in essence, the conditional release of an offender from criminal liability for the purpose of handing him over for communal re-education (at his place of work) to a collective which has interceded for him. It assumes that:

(a) the crime committed is not of any great social danger, nor accompanied by grave consequences;

(b) it is a first offence;

(c) the offender's guilt is established;

(d) the offender genuinely repents;

(e) the character of the offence and of the offender suggests the possibility of effective communal 'correction' (thus such probation cannot be extended twice);

(f) a genuine intercession on the offender's behalf has been made by the collective at his place of work, study or residence and adopted by it by a two-thirds majority.[54]

So far as those who have custody of the offender—whether court, prosecutor, investigator or militia—are concerned, any transference to collective probation is an *ex gratia* act and not an obligation. It does differ from the comrades' courts procedure in that it can only be brought into operation where a criminal offence has been committed. Soviet legal opinion differs as to whether or not communal probation is an act of criminal punishment[55]—the official line of thought appears to be that it is not.[56] On this hypothesis there is little difficulty in explaining away the fact that the offender can be surrendered to probation even before he has been taken to court.[57] It can also be argued that once the fact of the crime has been established and the offender has repented, there is no need to prove the element of guilt. As one authority has revealingly put it:

'If the guilt of the person in committing the crime or the event of the crime is not evident . . . the initiation of criminal proceedings and the performance of a preliminary investigation are obligatory.'[58]

It has been complained that this procedure is used 'to save a person from a well-deserved punishment'.[59]

Having been put on collective probation, the offender is released from it after one year if 'he has demonstrated his correction by his honest attitude to labour and his exemplary conduct in everyday life'; if he has not done so on the expiring of this period, or has abused the trust of the collective at any time during that period, his case is referred back to the court or the prosecutor for proceedings to be reinstituted as appropriate.[60]

Druzhinniks

The *druzhinniks* are a form of unpaid, voluntary detachments of worker's militia which originally started up in a number of Leningrad factories at the end of 1958,[61] and the initiative was followed at Ryazan, Gorlovka, Enakievo, Saratov and Penza. Initially there was a great deal of confusion over titles; it was some months before they came to be generally known as *druzhinniks* and over a year and a half before their powers and functions were properly regularised.[62] The RSFSR Regulations on them provide that:

(a) their functions are preventive, i.e. to patrol public places, etc.;

(b) they must not be under 18;

(c) they are organised under a *raion* or town headquarters staff;

(d) they have the right to demand citizens' identification papers; to draw up signed statements; to escort offenders to their headquarters or to the militia;

(e) they wear badges or armbands.

In 1965, there were more than 5½ million *druzhinniks* in the

USSR (organised into 130,000 *druzhinas*).[63] Figures for 1964 show that there were four million in the RSFSR,[64] of whom Moscow accounted for about 248,000.[65] However, these impressive numbers include people whose presence was a formality or who had been persuaded to 'volunteer'.[66] There was evidence in 1966 that local Party organisations were purging the ranks of the *druzhinniks*.[67]

Druzhinniks are relatively circumscribed. They are not entitled to wear or use arms. They have no power of arrest or fine. But the rationale under which they operate is that they shall not be too closely identified with nor in any way subordinate to the militia.[68] In this sense they diverge from the so-called Brigades for Assisting the Militia which they appear to have replaced. Nevertheless in practice the demarcation line is not always hard and fast: their headquarters staff on occasion include specific militia assistants.[69]

They do have some effective sanctions; they are supposed to keep a check on 'crime-prone' and parasitic elements and to bring moral pressure to bear on them; if this fails they refer the case to court.[70] They can be called on to help with policing at mass demonstrations, meetings, etc.:[71] 'the *druzhinniks* take over the guarding of the enterprise during the mass Sunday voluntary stint of workers and employees'.[72] Although the *druzhinniks* are an effective adjunct to the forces of law and order, their somewhat anomalous rôle causes them on occasion to be the prosecutors of perfectly law-abiding citizens and there have been several cases of *druzhinniks* abusing their powers. Violent resistance offered to a *druzhinnik* (and to a militiaman) has been punishable with up to one year's deprivation of freedom under the law of February 15, 1962, which also prescribed the death penalty for an attempt on the life of a *druzhinnik* when performing his civic duties. The *druzhinniks* are in fact at best a useful batch of auxiliary policemen and at worst an army of unpaid vigilantes.

OTHER FORMS OF PUBLIC PARTICIPATION

Public participation in the discharge of justice over recent years has assumed a wide variety of new forms. One of the earliest and most disputed manifestations of this trend was the introduction in the Union Republics between 1957 and 1959 of a series of laws on 'anti-social parasitic elements' which ran directly counter to the principle enumerated in the Bases of Criminal Judicial Procedure of December, 1958, that:[73]

'no one may be pronounced guilty of the commission of a crime and subjected to criminal punishment other than by sentence of the court'.

In the event there was a considerable body of legal opinion opposed to these laws and the RSFSR Draft Law published in August, 1957, was not enacted until May, 1961, and then in a substantially amended form. This gave the other Union Republics the opportunity to amend accordingly the more drastic versions which they themselves had already enacted at varying dates from February, 1958. However, even in their post-1961 amended form these laws still provided for the following:

(a) action against 'parasites' could be initiated either by People's Courts or by 'collectives' of factories, farms, etc. (the collective acting as tribunal in the latter case);

(b) a two-thirds attendance on the part of the collective was a valid quorum and sentence was by majority public vote;

(c) sentence of from two to five years exile with compulsory labour could be passed, subject only to confirmation by the local Soviet Executive Committee;

(d) the accused could be brought along by force if necessary; he had no defence counsel nor any right of appeal; he could not be present during the actual voting.

In 1965, the RSFSR Supreme Soviet considerably altered this extra-judicial law.[74] The most important change was to make the Soviet Executive Committee the competent authority for action against parasites (except in Moscow, the Moscow region and Leningrad, where People's Courts were to perform this function). Thus provisions (a) and (b) above were radically altered. Secondly the local Soviets were obliged to exile people to nearby areas for an unspecified period (although they could be sent to 'places specially provided' from Moscow and Leningrad, specifically for a period of two to five years). This modification presumably came as a result of many complaints from the remote areas to which parasites had been exiled and where they had continued in their old way of life, corrupted the local population, etc.

Provision (d) remains in force. Other aspects of the revised law continue to give grounds for disquiet.

Definitions of 'idler' and 'parasite' are still not precise. (It has been revealed that alcoholics, those in need of medical treatment—even schizophrenics—were exiled under the terms of the former decree.[75]) The Executive Committees have been granted considerable discretionary powers; their decisions may not be protested by the procuracy. The differentiated procedures involving offenders in the Moscow and Leningrad areas and those elsewhere are anomalous; it is curious that no time limits relating to the latter offenders were stipulated.

The only article of the former law to remain unchanged is the one which provides irrefutable proof of the extra-legality of the law: if any offences punishable in criminal law are disclosed during the initial check-up by the militia, the case must be passed to the prosecutor to institute proceedings. Thus the whole body of 'parasite' regulations falls outside the sphere of statutory crime.

Other forms of public involvement are many and varied. At the pre-trial stage they include (apart from *druzhinniks*):

(a) Communal assistant prosecutors and voluntary assistant investigators. These are deemed to be an indirect continuation of the groups for assisting the Prosecutor's Office which were officially disbanded in 1939.[76] Currently they help to collect evidence connected with the investigation of a given crime but are not supposed to be used to interrogate witnesses, conduct searches, etc.— though there have been proposals to widen their terms of reference.[77] They are recruited from 'workers, engineers, law students, old age pensioners, etc'.[78]

At the stage of court proceedings, other 'public' representatives with semi-official status are:

(b) 'Communal defenders' and 'communal prosecutors' who are 'spontaneously' delegated by the accused's collective (at his factory or organisation, etc.) to support or oppose him on their collective behalf and are admitted to the trial at the court's discretion.[79] They function parallel to but separate from the 'professional' counsel for the defence and the prosecution.[80] They have the right to take part in the trial, and they possess equal status to all the other partners to the trial.[81] They can cross-question, analyse the evidence and even comment on what sanctions should be applied; their rôle is to be 'the spokesmen of public opinion *vis-à-vis* the given case'.[82]

On March 26, 1960, the Supreme Court condemned the practice of permitting a 'communal defender' as well as a 'communal prosecutor' from the same organisation to act with regard to the same defendant.[83] (The resultant absurdity, i.e. that one person speaks in the name of an entire 'collective', which is frequently divided over the issue, has given rise to comment.[84]) Their presence can, of course, work either way—towards strengthening either the prosecution or the defence. (In the first half of 1966, 'communal prosecutors' took part in nearly 13 per cent of all criminal cases, while 'communal defenders' only took part in seven per cent.[85]) They certainly tend to introduce further extra-legal elements: one senior official of the Prosecutor's Office inferred that the delegation of communal defenders to speak up for patently guilty offenders was a form of double insurance practised by various collectives.[86] From this it is not far to the argument that the public ought not to be seen defending the guilty. Also, certain inequities have been pointed out, e.g. the fact that two 'prosecutors' are ranged against one defence counsel[87] every time a 'communal prosecutor' is involved in a case.

Other bodies which operate more remotely from the judicial system include:

(c) The Permanent Commissions for the Protection of Socialist Legality (the titles of which exhibit minor differences from town to town) attached to the local Soviets which were mostly instituted after the XX Party Congress. These commissions keep in close touch with the *druzhinniks*, the comrades' courts, the house committees, the militia and other State and public organisations. They review such questions as the working of the internal passport system, the custody of juvenile offenders, and the observance of the relevant directives issued by the Executive Committee of the local Soviet. One action taken by the Moscow City Commission was to arrange in May, 1961, for the militia organs to clear all the Moscow railway stations of tramps and beggars by either putting them to work or evicting them from the city.[88]

(d) Street Committees and Housing Block Committees and (in certain rural districts) Councils of Elders—these and similar communal bodies act as primary filters. Their functions include checking up on the observation of the internal passport system, uncovering malingerers and disturbances of public order. They can notify cases of anti-social conduct to the proper authorities and they pass on information about petty theft of public property.[89] There are even apartment blocks 'of Communist conduct,' the residents in which undertake to:

'actively participate in the communal life of the block, maintain exemplary order in the flats, prevent any instances of relations departing from the norm from occurring between neighbours, and actively struggle with the survivals of capitalism'.[90]

(e) Observer Commissions, established by Soviet Executive Committees; their members (who may not be lawyers or members of the public order organs, procuracy or courts) are proposed by 'public organisations' and 'collectives' of workers. They possess considerable powers of supervision over corrective labour establishments and other penal organs with the aim of ensuring that the correct punishment régime is being served and that the labour education, etc., of offenders is proceeding properly. They are supposed to keep an eye on those who have served their sentences,* help them with jobs (to judge from frequent Soviet comment there is considerable scope for their aid in this respect), housing, etc. The Observer Commissions possess certain rights, e.g. of demanding the necessary documents from the penal authorities, of examining offenders' complaints and petitioning for pardons or asking the courts for one of various forms of reduction or amelioration of sentence (jointly with the penal authorities or without them, depending on the specific nature of the desired change).[92] A member of the Prosecutor's Office who supervises penal institutions is present at sessions of the Observer Commissions. However, he is not entitled to interfere in their work and may only step in when legality has been infringed. He is also supposed to react to errors of omission.[93]

---

* 1966 regulations introducing 'administrative supervision' by the militia over certain categories of released offenders[91] was a further tacit admission, however, of the virtues of professionalism in combating crime.

[125]

SOURCES

1. *Sovetsky Ugolovny Protsess*, p. 12.
2. Karev, *Organizatsiya Suda i Prokuratury*, p. 44.
3. Tadevosyan, p. 75.
4. Lebedinsky and Kalenov, pp. 54–5.
5. *Sovetskoye Gosudarstvo i Pravo*, No. 3, 1960, p. 20 (Gorkin).
6. Dobrovolskaya, p. 6.
7. *Izvestiya*, May 28, 1939 (Decree of the Central Committee of the All-Union Communist Party (Bolsheviks) and of the Council of People's Commissars of the USSR).
8. *Vestnik Moskovskogo Universiteta*, No. 11, 1950.
9. *Ibid.*
10. *Ibid.*
11. Malyarov, p. 47; *Sotsialisticheskaya Zakonnost*, No. 2, 1967, p. 18 (Yakovlev).
12. *Sovetskaya Yustitsiya*, No. 11, 1966, p. 1.
13. *Entsiklopedichesky Slovar Pravovykh Znanii*, p. 245.
14. *Novoye Ugolovnoye Zakonodatelstvo RSFSR*, p. 23.
15. *Pravda Ukrainy*, February 6, 1953.
16. *Entsiklopedichesky Slovar Pravovykh Znanii*, p. 112.
17. *Sovetskoye Gosudarstvo i Pravo*, No. 10, 1965, p. 102 (Shafir).
18. *Partiinaya Zhizn*, No. 13, 1957, p. 54.
19. *Pravda*, December 13, 1964.
20. *Ibid.*, January 7, 1965.
21. *Partiinaya Zhizn*, No. 21, 1957, p. 22.

22. *Dvadtsat Vtoroi Syezd KPSS i Voprosy Ideologicheskoi Raboty*, pp. 236–7.
23. *Pravda*, January 23, 1962, and Verchenko, pp. 60–1. For other instances *see Pravda*, January 12, 1962 (Pskov *oblast*), and Lilin, pp. 12–16 (Yaroslavl, Kaluga and Omsk); *and also Partiinaya Zhizn*, No. 11, 1962, pp. 46–50.
24. *Partiinaya Zhizn*, No. 3, 1967, p. 31 (Sdobnov); *Izvestiya*, June 30, 1966 (Perlov); Kriger, p. 225.
25. *Sotsialisticheskaya Zakonnost*, No. 4, 1962, pp. 32–3 (Feofanov).
26. *Partiinaya Zhizn*, No. 24, 1965, p. 46 (Belsky).
27. e.g. *Byulleten Verkhovnogo Suda SSSR*, No. 6, 1966, pp. 14, 17, 19 (*re* hooliganism). *See also* the instructive passages in Feifer, pp. 248–50.
28. *Sovetskoye Gosudarstvo i Pravo*, No. 11, 1966, p. 43 (Chugunov and Gorsky).
29. Tadevosyan, p. 55.
30. *Sorok Let Sovetskogo Prava*, p. 565.
31. e.g. *Izvestiya*, March 15, 1966 (Koronevsky and Sukhodolets); *Literaturnaya Gazeta*, July 5, 1966 (Strogovich).
32. Yudelson, p. 26.
33. Galkin, pp. 250–1.
34. *Vedomosti Verkhovnogo Soveta RSFSR*, No. 26, 1961, art. 371 (Edict of the Presidium of the RSFSR Supreme Soviet of July 3, 1961).
35. Vorozheikin, p. 53.

36. *Sovetskoye Gosudarstvo i Pravo*, No. 4, 1965, pp. 159–60 (Mikhailovskaya).

37. *Ibid.*, No. 1, 1966, pp. 133–134 (Yakovlev, Kunitsky); *ibid.*, No. 6, 1967, pp. 112–113 (Martyanov); *Sovetskaya Yustitsiya*, No. 19, 1965, pp. 21–2 (Zavyalov) proposes a new (public) organ to check decisions on appeal.

38. *Sovetskaya Rossiya*, October 24, 1963.

39. *Vedomosti Verkhovnogo Soveta RSFSR*, No. 4, 1965, art. 83.

40. *Sovetskoye Gosudarstvo i Pravo*, No. 12, 1959, p. 108 (Savitsky).

41. Sokolov, p. 155; Berezovskaya, pp. 224–5; *Tovarishcheskiye Sudy*, p. 57. (Counter view expressed by Martinovich in *Sovetskoye Gosudarstvo i Pravo*, No. 10, 1965, p. 114).

42. Galkin, p. 249.

43. Sokolov, p. 155.

44. Vorozheikin, p. 36.

45. *Izvestiya*, February 21, 1967 (Gurbatov).

46. *Sovetskaya Yustitsiya*, No. 16, 1964, p. 15 (Sladkov).

47. Vorozheikin, pp. 39–40.

48. *Literaturnaya Gazeta*, January 25, 1967 (Bondarin and Cherny).

49. Dementyev, p. 56; and *Trud*, May 6, 1964.

50. *Novoye Ugolovnoye Zakonodatelstvo RSFSR*, p. 149.

51. Chermensky, p. 11.

52. *Sovetskaya Yustitsiya*, No. 6, 1967, p. 6.

53. Domakhin and Stepanov, p. 7.

54. *Nauchno-Praktichesky Kommentarii UPK RSFSR*, p. 37.

55. *Sovetskaya Yustitsiya*, No. 9, 1959, pp. 22–4 (Perlov), No. 12, 1959, pp. 62–4, and No. 3, 1960, p. 51.

56. *Sovetskoye Gosudarstvo i Pravo*, No. 2, 1960, pp. 24–5 (Romashkin); and Brainin, pp. 268–9.

57. *Sovetskaya Yustitsiya*, No. 11, 1959, p. 53 (Viktorov).

58. Mendelson, p. 60.

59. *Tovarishcheskiye Sudy*, pp. 142–3.

60. *Nauchno-Praktichesky Kommentarii UPK RSFSR*, p. 40.

61. Dementyev, p. 28.

62. Regulatory Order on the RSFSR Voluntary Detachments for the Protection of Public Order, approved by the Buro of the C.C. for the RSFSR and the RSFSR Council of Ministers, March 30, 1960 (*Sovetskaya Yustitsiya*, No. 5, 1960, pp. 30–32).

63. *Partiinaya Zhizn*, No. 20, 1965, p. 20 (Tikunov).

64. *Sovetskoye Gosudarstvo i Pravo*, No. 6, 1964, p. 6.

65. *Byulleten Ispolnitelnogo Komiteta Moskovskogo Gorodskogo Soveta Deputatov Trudyashchikhsya*, No. 22, November, 1964, p. 23.

66. *Izvestiya*, April 21, 1966 (Tikunov).

67. *Sovetskoye Gosudarstvo i Pravo*, No. 11, 1966, p. 11 (Nikitin).

68. Sokolov, p. 102.

69. *Sovetskaya Yustitsiya*, No. 16, 1964, p. 22.

70. *Ibid.*, p. 19.

71. Dementyev, p. 30.
72. *Ibid.*
73. December, 1958, Bases of Criminal Judicial Procedure, art. 7.
74. *Vedomosti Verkhovnogo Soveta RSFSR*, No. 38, 1965, pp. 737–9.
75. *Komsomolskaya Pravda*, November 16, 1965.
76. Berezovskaya, p. 39.
77. *Ibid.*, p. 198; and *Sovetskoye Gosudarstvo i Pravo*, No. 11, 1964, pp. 76–8 (Savitsky); *Problemy Iskoreniya Prestupnosti*, p. 145. For an opposed viewpoint, *see Sotsialisticheskaya Zakonnost*, No. 1, 1967, p. 23 (Savitsky).
78. *Izvestiya*, November 3, 1964.
79. *Nauchno-Praktichesky Kommentarii UPK RSFSR*, pp. 406–10.
80. *Ibid.*, pp. 452–3.
81. *Ibid.*, p. 452.
82. *Ibid.*, p. 453.
83. *Entsiklopedichesky Slovar Pravovykh Znanii*, p. 275.
84. *Izvestiya*, September 1, 1965 (Speer).
85. *Sovetskoye Gosudarstvo i Pravo*, No. 1, 1967, p. 43 (Anashkin). It has been claimed more than once, however, that the relationship is the other way about, e.g. *Izvestiya*, September 1, 1965 (Speer).
86. *Moskovskaya Pravda*, September 2, 1964; Tikunov in *Izvestiya*, April 21, 1966.
87. *Izvestiya*, September 1, 1965 (Speer).
88. Sokolov, p. 90.
89. *Ibid.*, pp. 64–5.
90. *Ibid.*, p. 71.
91. *Vedomosti Verkhovnogo Soveta SSSR*, No. 30, 1966, pp. 588–91.
92. RSFSR Statute on Observer Commissions, *Vedomosti Verkhovnogo Soveta RSFSR*, No. 40, 1965, pp. 803–7. For certain republican differences, *see Entsiklopedichesky Slovar Pravovykh Znanii*, p. 237.
93. Malyarov, pp. 168–170.

VI

Codification and Statistics

Codification has not been the strong point of Soviet jurisprudence. This has not been entirely the fault of Soviet jurists; important contributory factors have been, as already noted, the existence of special acts and procedures in direct contradiction with normative principles, and, more fundamentally, the twists and turns taken by Party ideology on the subject of the rôle of law, if any, in a Socialist society.

This lag in codification had been particularly marked since 1930. In 1965, it was stated that:

'Over 400,000 legislative acts and Government decisions, which have not yet been systematically arranged, have been published since the USSR was established. Since 1927 the publication ceased not only of a systematic collection of the legislation in force, but even of a chronological one.'[1]

All aspects of the law, not only criminal law, were affected. Between the publication of the USSR Constitution in 1936 and December, 1958, the only new codifying enactments to emerge were the 1938 Judiciary Act,[2] the May, 1955, Regulations on Supervision by Prosecutors[3] and the February, 1957, Regulations on the USSR Supreme Court.[4] During this period not a single Code was published, despite the ever-growing need. The decree of July, 1936, setting up the USSR People's Commissariat of Justice and the 1936 Constitution both focused attention on this anomaly. The previous Criminal Code had dated back to 1926,[5] and work undertaken in 1939 to draft a new one had not seen the light of day.[6]

Since about 1959 some of the leeway has been made up. The Union Republics brought out their Criminal Codes in the period May, 1959–December, 1961.[7] Even this implied an unduly long time lag between their publication and the prior emergence of the December, 1958, Bases—a fact which had not escaped comment in the RSFSR.[8]

Similar progress has been made with the introduction of new

Codes of Criminal Procedure,[9] a new RSFSR Civil Code,[10] the partial amendment of the RSFSR Civil Procedure Code,[11] and a new Regulatory Order on Defence Lawyers.[12] Nevertheless a lot still remains to be done, not only in such relatively tranquil spheres as that of the Land Code[13] but also in those of the Labour Code[14] (dating back to 1922) and of the Corrective Labour Code. Despite the total obsolescence of the last major corrective labour law, dating back to 1930,[15] and despite the accumulation of a considerable volume of partly contradictory legislation on the subject since 1954, no visible progress has been made (although in 1966 it was claimed that draft Bases of Corrective Labour Law had been worked out for the USSR and the Union Republics[16]). This is not for want of pressure on the part of Soviet lawyers.[17] Indeed it has been suggested that some theorists, not content with altering old codes, are always itching to revise the new ones.[18]

Just as the working out of codes was in part complicated by the presence of contradictory acts, so the absence of such codes contributed its share towards the accumulation of irregularities, anomalies and obsolete norms. The consequences were all but chaotic; as was stated in 1957,[19] they included:

(a) failure to repeal or amend old acts when issuing new ones;

(b) the annulling or amending of previous acts in an insufficiently specific form;

(c) the introduction by non-normative acts of amendments to normative ones;

(d) the inclusion of long-term general rulings into fixed-term orders or acts;

(e) contradictions arising from the failure to co-ordinate the contents and drafting of acts concerning one and the same subject;

(f) complex, diffuse formulation of acts;

(g) the plugging of gaps in criminal law by USSR Supreme Court rulings and by current court practice.

Similar complaints were being voiced in 1965.[20]

Behind all this lay the attitude, with which Vyshinsky for one was associated, that if a law 'lagged behind life' it should be simply discarded, on which subsequent comment was:

'The proclaiming of the possibility of laying a law aside and perceiving in this the dialectic in the development of Soviet law or a struggle against juridical fetichism is tantamount to justifying any illegality or arbitrariness under the slogan of alleged expediency.'[21]

The disavowal of Vyshinsky has by no means solved all the problems. Lack of co-ordination between the various kinds of normative acts issued by the USSR Supreme Soviet and its Presidium and the USSR Council of Ministers as well as by other bodies continues to present problems.[22] There are still frequent complaints of inadequate demarcation and correlation of All-Union legislation and Republican legislation.[23] One official complaint was that the RSFSR Criminal Code had been the subject of no fewer than three authoritative but contradictory analyses published in Moscow, Leningrad and Sverdlovsk respectively.[24]

Although there have been indications that a collection of RSFSR legislation in force has been prepared by the Juridical Commission attached to the USSR Council of Ministers—the body to which this task was entrusted[25]—two authorities have drawn attention to some of the important issues which need to be resolved before such a work could itself be accepted as the official text of all legislation in force.[26] The same writers also referred to secret legislation, among other categories of law in force, which should not be included even in such a 'complete' collection.[27]

Other difficulties hinder the uniform and rational application of the law. As the USSR Prosecutor-General wrote in 1956:

'In a number of cases various relations are regulated by numerous derivative acts, some of which are not known at all, not only to scientific but frequently to practical workers too, and this leads to wrong decisions, to the infringement of the rights of citizens and gives rise to contradictory practices. There can be no serious talk whatsoever about the propagation of Soviet legislation if the systematised collections of laws are only published on a restricted circulation basis and are available only to a limited number of officials.'[28]

and,

'It was rightly pointed out at the XX Congress of the Party that many theoretical works bear a speculative and abstract character because of the unnecessary secrecy of statistical data. This applies with full force to scientific works on legal subjects. The few legal works which use statistical data usually quote them for the period not later than the 1930s when collections were published by the Institute of Criminal Policy of the Prosecutor's Office of the USSR and other works appeared the authors of which had the possibility of using such data. In the subsequent period such legal works completely ceased to appear in our country.'[29]

A year after Rudenko's article another article by an *oblast* prosecutor appeared in the same journal. He stated:

'Legal scientific workers usually judge crime on the basis of individual criminal cases, reports of trials published in the periodical press. This is largely to be explained by the fact that obstacles are placed in the way of access to statistical information.'[30]

Since then the position has partially improved. On the one hand though the publication of the legislation of the USSR Supreme Soviet and its Presidium has continued uninterrupted, the corresponding legislation of the USSR Council of Ministers and the USSR Ministries has since 1949 only been available in a restricted publication. The relevant law of June 19, 1958,[31] does not touch on the orders issued by governmental bodies.

On the purely statistical side, the position is the same. The 30 years' lag since 1930[32] is taking a lot of catching up. One promising organisational sign has been the creation in 1963 of the All-Union Institute for the Study of the Reasons for and the Elaboration of Preventive Measures against Crime.[33] The Institute also co-ordinates criminological research by academic and scientific institutions;[34] detailed investigations have been conducted in recent years. An experimental course in criminology at university level was introduced in 1963,[35] and in 1964 a CPSU Central Committee decree on higher level education stated that this would be among the disciplines introduced into the syllabuses of the appropriate juridical educational establishments.[36]

In 1966, after pointed criticism of the prevailing system of statistical returns,[37] a revised, standardised statistical system was introduced.[38] By paying particular attention to unsolved crimes, it was apparently hoped to avoid the (much criticised) abuses resulting from previous concentration on cases successfully solved.[39] Presumably Soviet scholars will now be permitted to become acquainted with such statistics; this has not been the case in the recent past.[40] There still seems to be a marked shying away from publicly giving any sort of statistics for crimes or criminals in the USSR: this is on occasion highlighted by the readiness with which foreign criminal statistics are quoted and contrasted with Soviet indices expressed in percentages.[*][41] One of the earliest caveats against undue absorption in statistical research was that uttered by Lenin:

'Statistics should illustrate the social-economic relationships which have been brought to light by a comprehensive analysis, but must not turn into an end in itself.'[45]

Now that statistics have been rehabilitated, Soviet researchers are also beginning to explore the sociological, psychological and biological factors in crime. This widening of the horizons is the subject of keen debate. The disingenuous ascription of crime in the USSR to the 'influence of bourgeois propaganda' is now only maintained by a minority.

SOURCES

1. *Izvestiya*, September 7, 1965 (Chkhikvadze).
2. Law of August 16, 1938 (*Vedomosti Verkhovnogo Soveta SSSR*, No. 11, 1938).
3. Edict of Presidium of USSR Supreme Soviet of May 24, 1955 (*Vedomosti Verknovnogo Soveta SSSR*, No. 9, 1955).
4. Law of February 12, 1957 (*Vedomosti Verkhovnono Soveta SSSR*, No. 4, 1957).
5. RSFSR *Laws*, 1926, 80: 600.
6. *Sorok Let Sovetskogo Prava*, p. 498.
7. *Ugolovnoye Zakonodatelstvo Soyuza SSR i Soyuznykh Respublik*, vol. 1, pp. 647–55, and vol. 2, pp. 629–

639: respective enactment dates are—RSFSR, October 27, 1960; Ukraine, December 28, 1960; Belorussia, December 29, 1960; Uzbekistan, May 21, 1959; Kazakhstan, July 22, 1959; Georgia, December 30, 1960; Azerbaidzhan, December 8, 1960; Lithuania, June 26, 1961; Moldavia, March 24, 1961; Latvia, January 6, 1961; Kirgizia, December 29, 1960; Tadzhikistan, August 17, 1961; Armenia, March 7, 1961; Turkmenistan, December 22, 1961; and Estonia, January 6, 1961.
8. *Novoye Ugolovnoye Zakonodatelstvo RSFSR*, p. 163.

[*] A rough-and-ready estimate of the number of criminal cases brought to court can nevertheless be deduced (the caveat being, on Soviet admissions themselves, that this index does not reflect the degree of criminality[42]). In 1965, it was stated that civil cases comprise about 85 per cent of all court cases.[43] The number of civil actions in 1964 was said to be 2,202,032.[44] In round figures therefore, the number of criminal cases in 1964 was 330,000.

9. *Vedomosti Verkhovnogo Soveta RSFSR*, No. 40, 1960, art. 588 (RSFSR Law of October 27, 1960).

10. *Vedomosti Verkhovnogo Soveta RSFSR*, No. 24, 1964, art. 416 (Edict of the Presidium of the RSFSR Supreme Soviet of June 12, 1964).

11. *Vedomosti Verkhovnogo Soveta RSFSR*, No. 1940, 1960, art. 597 (RSFSR Law of October 27, 1960, ratifying Edict of Presidium of RSFSR Supreme Soviet of October 5, 1960).

12. *Ibid.*, No. 29, 1962, art. 450 (RSFSR Law of July 25, 1962).

13. RSFSR *Laws*, 1922, 68: 901.

14. RSFSR *Laws*, 1922, 70: 903.

15. USSR *Laws*, 1930, 22:248.

16. *Ispravitelno-Trudovoe Pravo*, p. 49; *Sotsialisticheskaya Zakonnost*, No. 9, 1966, p. 18 (the draft 'is being worked out').

17. Belyaev, pp. 20–1.

18. *Novoye Ugolovnoye Zakonodatelstvo RSFSR*, p. 206.

19. *Sorok Let Sovetskogo Prava*, pp. 50–1 and 499.

20. *Izvestiya*, September 7, 1965 (Chkhikvadze).

21. *Sovetskoye Gosudarstvo i Pravo*, No. 12, 1957, p. 20.

22. *Sovetskoye Gosudarstvo i Pravo*, No. 1, 1956, pp. 4–5; and *Novoye Ugolovnoye Zakonodatelstvo RSFSR*, p. 186.

23. Brainin, pp. 49–50.

24. *Sovetskaya Yustitsiya*, No. 18, 1964, p. 2 (leading article).

25. *Pravda*, May 18, 1967 (Dicharov).

26. *Sovetskoye Gosudarstvo i Pravo*, No. 9, 1966, pp. 52–58 (Samoshchenko and Shebanov).

27. *Ibid.*, pp. 56–7.

28. *Sovetskoye Gosudarstvo i Pravo*, No. 3, 1956, p. 20.

29. *Ibid.*, p. 20.

30. *Sovetskoye Gosudarstvo i Pravo*, No. 3, 1957, p. 45.

31. *Vedomosti Verkhovnogo Soveta SSSR*, No. 14, 1958.

32. *Sovetskoye Gosudarstvo i Pravo*, No. 11, 1959, p. 64 (Utevsky); *ibid.*, No. 11, 1966, p. 76; *Problemy Iskoreniya Prestupnosti*, pp. 29–30. Sakharov, p. 25 (*re* criminal psychology); Ostroumov, p. 78.

33. *Sovetskaya Yustitsiya*, No. 18, 1964, p. 2 (leading article); and *Sovetskoye Gosudarstvo i Pravo*, No. 5, 1964, p. 5 (Kudryavtsev).

34. *Entsiklopedichesky Slovar Pravovykh Znanii*, p. 208.

35. *Sovetskoye Gosudarstvo i Pravo*, No. 11, 1964, p. 92 (Ostroumov and Kusnetsova).

36. *Izvestiya*, August 4, 1964. Malyarov, p. 309.

37. e.g. *Problemy Iskoreniya Prestupnosti*, pp. 38, 49, 51–2; *Sovetskoye Gosudarstvo i Pravo*, No. 9, 1965, pp. 102–3 (Shlyapochnikov).

38. *Sotsialisticheskaya Zakonnost*, No. 1, 1967, pp. 34–7 (Ostroumov and Panchenko).

39. *Ibid.*, p. 35. For the abuses of the previous system, *see*,

for example, *Sovetskaya Rossiya*, May 21, 1966 (Protopopov).

40. *Sotsialisticheskaya Zakonnost*, No. 8, 1962, p. 96 (Panchenko).

41. e.g. the Chairman of the Criminal Collegium of the USSR Supreme Court in *Byulleten Verkhovnogo Suda SSSR*, No. 5, 1964, p. 17; *ibid.*, No. 2, 1966, p. 10 (slightly more frank).

42. *Sotsialisticheskaya Zakonnost*, No. 1, 1967, p. 36 (Ostroumov and Panchenko). For relevant comments on 'hidden' criminality, *see Problemy Iskoreniya Prestupnosti*, pp. 51–52.

43. *Izvestiya-Nedelya*, No. 2, 1965, p. 5 (Panyugin).

44. *Sovetskaya Rossiya*, December 4, 1964 (Leshchevsky).

45. Lenin, *Collected Works*, vol. 3, p. 506.

VII
Conflict and Debate

In the post-1934 period—the period during which legal nihilism receded into the background and law came to acquire respectability as a means for underpinning the Soviet régime and institutional system—the measure of freedom of expression allowed to Soviet legal theorists and members of the judiciary has closely reflected the measure and type of legality prescribed for Soviet justice by Party policy. It is only in recent times that Pashukhanis and Krylenko have been posthumously rehabilitated from their condemnation in 1938 as wreckers.[1] Vyshinsky could not have played the rôle of chief censor and official oracle had he not had official backing.

In fact, the admission of a perceptible measure of debate goes back no further than 1954. Such views as ran contrary to the 'received legal doctrine' that were expressed in post-war years tended to be denounced as anti-Marxist. Thus one 1951 review of a legal textbook by Cheltsov declared:

'The book does not show that Soviet criminal trial is based on Socialist legality and permeated with Socialist humanism. What is more, the author of the textbook suggests to the reader that in the Soviet State there is a neglectful attitude towards the interests of the individual.... Let us note that the expression of non-Marxist views is not something fortuitous for Professor Cheltsov. In his 1948 textbook he only repeats the wrong views which he expressed earlier and, in particular, in the same textbook in its edition of 1928 and 1929.... Let us note likewise that Comrade Cheltsov has never subjected his old non-Marxist views to criticism and never renounced them.'[2]

In such circumstances it was hardly to be expected of Soviet lawyers that they should seek to examine such delicate subjects as the procedural guarantees of the rights of the accused, incriminational trends among the judiciary and so forth. As has lately been said:

'Of course, such a state of affairs, when disagreement with the point of view of A. Ya. Vyshinsky was viewed as a departure from

[136]

Marxism-Leninism, as a "heresy", did not contribute to creative discussion, all the more so that individual errors in the field of theory or in practical activity were easily designated (in the conditions of the theory of the sharpening of the class struggle under Socialism) as sabotage.'[3]

The first signs of relaxation by the Party did not come until 1954 for, as was said two years later:

'The speech [at the XIX Party Congress in 1952] of A. N. Poskrebyshev engendered among some Soviet jurists an incorrect attitude to the elaboration of one of the most important questions of the theory of Socialist criminal law. The intervention of the Party Press was required to stress the importance of working out the problems of guilt in connection with the strengthening of Socialist legality (*Kommunist*, 1954, No. 5, pages 8–9) so that Soviet jurists could defend the correct positions in this question.'[4]

After the XX Party Congress in February, 1956, the time when the first direct attack on Vyshinsky's teachings on 'proofs' and 'confession' and 'absolute truth' was published,[5] the doors were opened much wider.

The consequence has been twofold. Not only has there been far-reaching discussion of Soviet jurisprudence, but there has also been a perceptible change of front in relation to bourgeois law and to pre-revolutionary Russian practice. Sentiments such as:

'The Soviet jurist expresses in all his activities a feeling of irreconcilability towards all manner of reactionary bourgeois "theories", towards despised cosmopolitanism and reverence for all things foreign.... In all exploiting States the activities of the courts are directed in the first place to the suppression, the terrorist intimidation of the exploited masses.'[6]

are no longer mandatory.

Soviet jurists are now largely able to take up differing positions on the subject.[7] Some authors still denounce the influence of the bourgeois conception of the rôle of defence counsel on their Soviet counterparts;[8] or hastily deny any fancied resemblance between Soviet and bourgeois appellate procedure.[9] On the other hand, many Soviet authorities now advocate the adoption of procedures or institutes bearing a close resemblance to those adopted abroad, and some of them go so far as indirectly to acknowledge their origin:

'The principal antithesis between Soviet and bourgeois law consists in the class this law subserves, in whose and which interests it protects and not in how it solves individual specific questions. Attempts to assert that on our side all is "the other way around" are simply harmful.'[10]

and,

'One should therefore regard as incorrect various attempts to pass off the utilisation of procedural forms already well known to mankind as the infiltration into Soviet procedural theory of "bourgeois-liberal institutes".'[11]

As has been indicated in previous chapters, Soviet lawyers and jurists have succeeded in registering many advances in theory and practice over the last few years. A number of these have been incorporated into the December, 1958, enactments; others will undoubtedly exert indirect influence on judicial practice. As is to be expected, not all Soviet lawyers and jurists favour reform in the direction of liberalisation, but the consensus of opinion among the Soviet legal profession appears to lean that way, and such major or minor reversals as take place largely have their source elsewhere.

The vexed question of the statute of analogy, introduced in the 1922 RSFSR Criminal Code, has now been settled in favour of its abandonment.*[12] Though views on the advisability of the statute of analogy had differed sharply from 1936 onwards and it had been left out of the draft Criminal Code that was discussed in 1940, wide use was made of it from 1941 to 1945, especially in USSR Supreme Court rulings.[13] In the post-war period analogy was used only infrequently. Its present abandonment is usually grounded on the argument that, contrary to what Vyshinsky said, a fully comprehensive Criminal Code can be drawn up.[14] However, a warning note needs to be sounded for, as has been pointed out,[15] most of the opponents of analogy appear to want to have their cake and eat it. They refrain from saying that some sacrifice of the power to punish socially dangerous acts not covered by law is desirable for the sake of strengthening legality, but imply that such power can

* The statute of analogy was based on article 16 of the previous RSFSR Criminal Code which laid down that:

'If one or other socially dangerous action is not directly provided for in the present Code, the basis and the extent of the liability for it shall be determined in relation to those articles in the Code which cover those crimes that are the most analogous to it in kind.'

be retained even without analogy. The balance of advantage means or should mean accepting with a good grace that:

'in a number of cases where socially dangerous actions are committed, these, not being provided for in the Criminal Code, must remain unpunishable as no one can ever create a code that will cover all socially dangerous actions'.[16]

In fact several authorities still argue that the norm-setting decisions of the USSR Supreme Court partake of analogy.[17]

Vyshinsky's teachings on the subject of guilt have been set aside;[18] his assertion that it was impossible for the courts to establish 'absolute truth' and that the establishment of 'relative truth', i.e. 'the maximum degree of probability in arriving at conviction of this truth', was adequate has suffered the same fate.[19] Another proposition that went hand-in-hand with the above was the acceptance of the confession of the accused as adequate proof of his guilt, even in the immediate absence of circumstantial proof;[20] as was stated in refutation of this approach in 1956:

'What conclusions some Soviet jurists have drawn from the incorrect statements of A. Ya. Vyshinsky on the question of the importance of the evidence of the accused can be judged by A. Vasiliev's article "Tactics in cross-examining the accused", published in the journal *Socialist Legality*, the organ of the Ministry of Justice of the USSR, the Supreme Court of the USSR and the Public Prosecutor's Office of the USSR. The author of this article gives special prominence to the question "of the importance of a proper corroboration of a confession by the accused of his guilt" (*Socialist Legality*, No. 4, 1950, p. 20). "The accused has confessed," writes A. Vasiliev, "that is a tremendous result, especially in a case where there is no direct evidence of the guilt of the accused. This is a great success for the investigator, but the outcome of the case is not settled by this. For a successful outcome of the case it is vital that this confession should give other evidence into the hands of the investigator and should be so corroborated that the accused feels himself tied by this confession and does not renounce it with ease under further cross-examination by the investigator and in court: the latter event is particularly tragic for the case." '[21]

The principle of the presumption of innocence has also been the subject of much debate.[22] One of the counter-arguments had amounted to saying that this principle was a good thing in the capitalist context but a bad thing in the Soviet one.[23] A prolonged polemic in 1964 even led to an unsuccessful civil action, brought by an opponent of this principle against a writer in *Izvestiya* and the newspaper's editorial board.[24] The

December, 1958, enactments now provide that the burden of proof lies on the prosecution.[25] This stops well short of the explicit proclamation of the principle that had been advocated by several leading jurists[26] and conversely attacked as an attempt 'to introduce into our theory and practice the decrepit dogmas of bourgeois law',[27] but is none the less a modest advance. A fundamental factor that in any case inhibits the full realisation of the principle of presumption of innocence is, as already noted, the peculiar rôle of the prosecutor and the presumption that any prosecution brought must be—or *per se* ought to be—the prosecution of guilty parties.

Another principle under dispute which is likely to come in for increasing attention is that of the factor of 'competitiveness' in trial procedure. In a sense this is yet another, though a cardinal, facet of the debate between the 'proceduralists' and the 'therapeutists'. The latter argue that 'competitiveness' is a feature of bourgeois procedure under which the defence, the prosecution and the court each plays a separate procedural rôle with a separate task and divergent interests but which is not acceptable to Soviet law under which the 'parties' to the trial have, or should have, complementary rôles.[28] Thus, hypothetically, the prosecutor is able to appeal against any unlawful sentence, even one of wrongful condemnation.[29] For their part, the proceduralists necessarily favour 'competitiveness' (even where they refrain from championing it demonstratively) since it is the conception which is consonant with greater procedural guarantees in all directions.[30]

There have also been hopeful signs of the Soviet legal profession rising to its own defence:[31] thus, several voices have even been raised against the practice of publishing condemnatory articles about cases before sentence has been passed.[32] Though the Chairman of the USSR Supreme Court has commented in similar terms,[33] political expediency may continue to dictate the appearance of such newspaper articles.[34] However, the inadmissibility of permitting court verdicts to be swayed by outside pressures[35]—including public opinion[36]—is also being increasingly pointed out. The champions of procedural guarantee are thus vocal and active. As one of them wrote:

'Any underestimation of procedural norms is anti-democratic *per se*. It forces judicial practice backwards to the times of arbitrary rule and illegality and contradicts the course set by the Party towards strengthening legality and the legal system.'[37]

SOURCES

1. *Sorok Let Sovetskogo Prava*, p. 512.
2. *Sovetskoye Gosudarstvo i Pravo*, No. 12, 1951, pp. 73–6.
3. *Sorok Let Sovetskogo Prava*, p. 590.
4. *Sovetskoye Gosudarstvo i Pravo*, No. 4, 1956, p. 28.
5. *Sovetskoye Gosudarstvo i Pravo*, No. 2, 1956, pp. 8–9.
6. Karev, *Sovetskoye Sudoustroistvo*, p. 14 and p. 20.
7. e.g. *Sovetskaya Yustitsiya*, No. 15, 1963, p. 30 (review of book by Shargorodsky).
8. Perlov, *Sudebnoye Sledstviye*, p. 126.
9. Kutsova, p. 25; and Cheltsov, p. 60.
10. *Sorok Let Sovetskogo Prava*, pp. 505–6—though there are official caveats from time to time.
11. Rakhunov, *Uchastniki Ugolovno-Protsessualnoi Deyatelnosti*, p. 75.
12. *Sovetskoye Gosudarstvo i Pravo*, No. 4, 1962, p. 13 (leading article).
13. *Sorok Let Sovetskogo Prava*, p. 526.
14. *Sovetskoye Gosudarstvo i Pravo*, No. 4, 1956, p. 30 (Piontkovsky and Chkhikvadze); Solovyev, pp. 19–20; *Sotsialisticheskaya Zakonnost*, No. 7, 1962, p. 11 (Piontkovsky); and Piontkovsky, p. 53.
15. *Sorok Let Sovetskogo Prava*, p. 529.
16. *Ibid.*, p. 532.
17. Dobrovolskaya, p. 94.
18. *Sorok Let Sovetskogo Prava*, pp. 523–4; *Sovetskoye Gosudarstvo i Pravo*, No. 4, 1956, p. 28. Some Soviet lawyers are said by their colleagues to remain unrepentant on this score, e.g. *Izvestiya*, May 25, 1962 (unsigned).
19. Aleksandrov, pp. 17–18; and *Sovetskoye Gosudarstvo i Pravo*, No. 4, 1956, p. 33 —but also *see Voprosy Sudoproizvodstva*, pp. 79–80; Dorokhov and Nikolaev, pp. 66–8; Rakhunov, *Uchastniki Ugolovno-Protsessualnoi Deyatelnosti*, pp. 105–6; and *Sovetskoye Gosudarstvo i Pravo*, No. 4, 1962, pp. 9–11 (leading article) for continuation of overall debate on this topic, one on which certain Soviet lawyers switched sides during and after the mid-fifties.
20. Lukashevich, p. 68.
21. *Kommunist*, No. 14, 1956, p. 53.
22. e.g. Lukashevich, pp. 42–58; *Kommunist*, No. 14, 1959, pp. 120–2 (Kudryavtsev *versus* Mokichev); *Voprosy Sudoproizvodstva*, pp. 69–70.
23. *Kommunist*, No. 14, 1959, p. 121 (Kudryavtsev *versus* Mokichev).
24. The sequence of events was as follows: *Literaturnaya Gazeta*, May 23, 1964: article by Strogovich on the presumption of innocence; *ibid.*, August 18, 1964, Filimonov, a district prosecutor, maintained that a defendant was already 'guilty from the point of view of

authority'; Strogovich rebutted this in the same issue; *Izvestiya*, September 10, 1964, carried a strong onslaught on Filimonov by Chaikovskaya; Filimonov then brought a civil action to vindicate his honour: *ibid.*, December 19, 1964. Additional comment by Gorkin (*ibid.*, December 2, 1964) and Strogovich, *Literaturnaya Gazeta*, December 17, 1964. Strogovich pointed out that Filimonov was only one of many prosecutors or investigators to hold such views. Chaikovskaya later published extracts from revealing letters received at the time (*Novy Mir*, No. 1, 1967, pp. 271–3).

25. December, 1958, Bases of Criminal Judicial Procedure, art. 14.

26. e.g. *Izvestiya*, March 27, 1958; *Voprosy Sudoproizvodstva*, p. 138; and Lukashevich, p. 43. Those for included: Perlov, Strogovich, Rakhunov, Kudryavtsev, Kaminskaya and Polyansky; those against included: Karev, Cheltsov, Tadevosyan, Mokichev and Golunsky.

27. *Pravda*, December 27, 1958 (Speech by Sharkov). Compare with Lukashevich, pp. 45–6.

28. *Voprosy Sudoproizvodstva*, pp. 124–6; *Sotsialisticheskaya Zakonnost*, No. 9,

1966, p. 34 (Kulikov and Zhogin).

29. *Ibid.*, p. 129.

30. Trusov, p. 138; *Literaturnaya Gazeta*, September 20, 1966 (Chetunova); *Izvestiya*, September 1, 1965 (Shpeer).

31. e.g. the discussion on communal probation (*Sovetskaya Yustitsiya*, No. 12, 1959, p. 64, as contrasted with *Sovetskoye Gosudarstvo i Pravo*, No. 5, 1963, p. 136).

32. e.g. Lukashevich, p. 149; *Sotsialisticheskaya Zakonnost*, No. 7, 1958, pp. 21–23; *Izvestiya*, June 30, 1966 (Perlov).

33. *Izvestiya*, December 2, 1964 (Gorkin).

34. e.g. the articles which appeared before the trial of Sinyavsky and Daniel: *Izvestiya*, January 13, 1966 (Eremin), and *Literaturnaya Gazeta*, January 22, 1966 (Kedrina), and numerous articles after the extensions of the death penalty in 1961–62.

35. *Izvestiya*, March 15, 1966 (Korenevsky and Sukhodolets); *Literaturnaya Gazeta*, July 5, 1966 (Strogovich).

36. e.g. *Izvestiya*, June 30, 1966 (Perlov); *Sovetskoye Gosudarstvo i Pravo*, No. 1, 1967, pp. 44–6 (Anashkin).

37. *Izvestiya*, February 9, 1962 (Bovin).

Conclusion

The value of any system of law to a Socialist society was once in question. This is the case no longer. Moreover, the improvement of the political climate in the Soviet Union in recent years has permitted a renewed emphasis on objective justice that was largely optional in the intervening years. However, the elements of political and social expediency still ultimately dictate the course taken by Soviet law.

Many tactical improvements have been effected both in practice and procedure; the extra-judicial institutions surviving from the period of Stalinism have been abolished. But Soviet law has a long way to travel yet and, eventually, its terminal point must by definition stop well short of the establishment of any rule of law. In the past it was the task of the protection of the Soviet régime and the obsession with the possibility of counter-revolution that were the inhibiting factors. In the immediate future it may be that the self-imposed task of transforming Soviet society and the consequent obsession with all the elements that get in the way of, or fail actively to contribute to, this transformation may prove an inhibiting factor of a less striking character but of even wider dimensions.

BIBLIOGRAPHY

Aleksandrov, N. G., *Primenenie Norm Sovetskogo Prava* (Application of the Norms of Soviet Socialist Law), Moscow University Publishing House, 1958.

Belyaev, N. A., *Predmet Sovetskogo Ispravitelno-Trudovogo Prava* (The Subject of Soviet Corrective Labour Law), Leningrad University Publishing House, 1960.

Berezovskaya, S. C., *Okhrana Prav Grazhdan Sovetskoi Prokuraturoi* (Protection of Citizens' Rights by the Soviet Prosecutor's Office), 'Science' Publishing House, Moscow, 1964.

Berman, H. J., Justice in Russia (An Interpretation of Soviet Law), Harvard University Press, Massachusetts, 1950.

Borodin, S. V., *Vybornost i Podotchetnost Narodnogo Suda* (Electivity and Accountability of the People's Court), State Publishing House of Juridical Literature, Moscow, 1957.

Brainin, Ya. M., *Ugolovnaya Otvetstvennost i ego Osnovaniye v Sovetskom Ugolovnom Prave* (Criminal Liability and its Foundation in Soviet Criminal Law), 'Juridical Literature' Publishing House, Moscow, 1963.

Byulleten Ispolnitelnogo Komiteta Moskovskogo Gorodskogo Soveta Deputatov Trudyashchikhsya (Bulletin of the Executive Committee of the Moscow City Soviet of Workers' Deputies), periodical, organ of the Executive Committee of the Moscow City Soviet.

Byulleten Verkhovnogo Suda SSSR (Bulletin of the USSR Supreme Court), periodical, organ of the USSR Supreme Court.

Chermensky, I. V., *Konets Tainoi Niti* (The End of a Secret Network), 'Knowledge' Publishing House, Moscow, 1965.

Dementyev, N. V., *Trudyashchiyesya na Strazhe Obshchestvennogo Poryadka* (The Workers On Guard over Public Order), All-Union Central Trade Union Council Publishing House, Moscow, 1959.

Dobrovolskaya, T. N., *Verkhovny Sud SSSR* (The USSR Supreme Court), Juridical Literature Publishing House, Moscow, 1964.

Domakhin, S. A., and Stepanov, V. G., *Obshchestvennoye Poruchitelstvo* (Communal Probation), State Publishing House of Juridical Literature, Moscow, 1962.

Dorokhov, V. Ya., and Nikolaev, V. S., *Obosnovannost Prigovora v Sovetskom Ugolovnom Protsesse* (The Basis of Sentencing in Soviet Criminal Law), State Publishing House of Juridical Literature, Moscow, 1959.

Dvadtsat Vtoroi Syezd KPSS i Voprosy Ideologicheskoi Raboty—Materialy Vsesoyuznogo Soveshchaniya po Voprosam Ideologicheskoi Raboty 25–28 Dekabrya 1961 (The Twenty-Second Congress of the CPSU and Questions of Ideological Work—Proceedings of the All-Union Conference on Questions of Ideological Work held on December 25–28, 1961), State Publishing House of Political Literature, Moscow, 1962.

Ekonomicheskaya Gazeta (Economic Gazette), weekly, organ of the Central Committee of the Communist Party of the Soviet Union.

Entsiklopedichesky Slovar Pravovykh Znanii (Encyclopedic Dictionary of Legal Knowledge), edited V. M. Chkhikvadze, S. N. Bratus, N. V. Zhogin, P. V. Kovanov, V. I. Terebilov, N. L. Tumanova; 'Soviet Encyclopedia' Publishing House, Moscow, 1965.

Feifer, George, *Justice in Moscow*, The Bodley Head, London, 1964.

Galkin, B. A., *Sovetsky Ugolovno-Protsessualny Zakon* (Soviet Criminal Procedural Law), State Publishing House of Juridical Literature, Moscow, 1962.

Gertsenzon, A. A., *Osnovnye Polozheniya Ugolovnogo Kodeksa RSFSR 1960 goda* (The Basic Principles of the RSFSR Criminal Code of 1960), State Publishing House of Juridical Literature, Moscow, 1961.

Gorshenin, K. P., *Sovetsky Sud* (The Soviet Court), State Publishing House of Juridical Literature, Moscow, 1957.

Gsovsky, V., Soviet Civil Law, 2 volumes, University of Michigan Law School, 1948.

Ispravitelno-Trudovoe Pravo (Corrective Labour Law), edited V. S. Tikunov, 'Juridical Literature' Publishing House, Moscow, 1966.

Izvestiya (News), newspaper, organ of the Presidium of the Supreme Soviet of the USSR.

Izvestiya-Nedelya (*Izvestiya*-Weekly), illustrated weekly supplement to *Izvestiya*.

Karev, D. S., *Organizatsiya Suda i Prokuratury v SSSR* (The Organisation of the Court and the Prosecutor's Office in the USSR), State Publishing House of Juridical Literature, Moscow, 1954.

Karev, D. S., *Sovetskoye Sudoustroistvo* (The Soviet Judicial System), State Publishing House of Juridical Literature, Moscow, 1951.

Karpets, I. I., *Individualizatsiya Nakazaniya v Sovetskom Ugolovnom Prave* (The Individualisation of Punishment in Soviet Criminal Law), State Publishing House of Juridical Literature, Moscow, 1961.

Kirichenko, V. F., *Vidy Dolzhnostnykh Prestuplenii po Sovetskomu Ugolovnomu Pravu* (Aspects of Malfeasance under Soviet Criminal Law), USSR Academy of Sciences Publishing House, Moscow, 1959.

Kommunist (The Communist), periodical, organ of the Central Committee of the Communist Party of the Soviet Union.

Kommunist Armenii (The Communist of Armenia), newspaper, organ of the Central Committee of the Communist Party of Armenia and of the Supreme Soviet and Council of Ministers of the Armenian SSR.

Kommunist Tadzhikistana (The Communist of Tadzhikistan), newspaper, organ of the Central Communist Party of Tadzhikistan and of the Supreme Soviet and Council of Ministers of the Tadzhik SSR.

Komsomolskaya Pravda (Young Communist Truth), newspaper, organ of the Central Committee of the *Komsomol*.

Korotkov, A. F., and Shind, V. I., *Obshchestvennost v Borbe s Narusheniyami Sotsialisticheskoi Zakonnosti* (The Public in the Struggle to Combat Infringements of Socialist Legality), State Publishing House of Juridical Literature, Moscow, 1962.

Kriger, G. A., *Borba s Khishcheniyami Sotsialisticheskogo Imushchestva* (The Struggle against Thefts of Socialist Property), 'Juridical Literature' Publishing House, Moscow, 1965.

Kursky, D. I., *Izbrannye Stati i Rechi* (Selected Articles and Speeches), State Publishing House of Juridical Literature, Moscow, 1948.

Kutsova, E. F., *Sovetskaya Kassatsiya Kak Garantiya Zakonnosti v Pravosudii* (Soviet Cassation as a Guarantee of Legality in Justice), State Publishing House of Juridical Literature, Moscow, 1957.

Lebedinsky, V. G., and Kalenov, Yu. A., *Prokurorsky Nadzor v SSSR* (Supervision by the Prosecutor in the USSR), State Publishing House of Juridical Literature, Moscow, 1957.

Leist, O. E., *Sanktsii v Sovetskom Prave* (Sanctions in Soviet Law), State Publishing House of Juridical Literature, Moscow, 1962.

Lenin, Collected Works (Fourth Edition), vols. 1–38, Lawrence and Wishart, London, 1960.

Lilyin, T., *Obshchestvennost i Ukrepleniye Zakonnosti* (The Public and the Strengthening of Legality), State Publishing House of Juridical Literature, Moscow, 1960.

Literaturnaya Gazeta (Literary Gazette), weekly, organ of the Board of the Union Writers of the USSR.

Lukashevich, V. Z., *Garantii Prav Obvinyaemogo v Sovetskom Ugolovnom Protsesse* (Guarantees of the Rights of the Accused in Soviet Criminal Procedure), Leningrad University Publishing House, 1959.

Malyarov, M. P. (editor), *Prokurorsky Nadzor v SSSR* (Supervision by the Prosecutor's Office in the USSR), 'Juridical Literature' Publishing House, Moscow, 1966.

Mendelson, G. A., *Peredacha na Poruki Lits Sovershivshikh Prestupleniya ne Predstavlyayushchiye Bolshoi Obshchestvennoi Opasnosti* (The Putting on Probation of Persons Who Have Committed Crimes Representing No Great Public Danger), Moscow University Publishing House, 1963.

Moskovskaya Pravda (Moscow Truth), newspaper, organ of the Moscow City Committee of the Communist Party of the Soviet Union, and of the Moscow Soviet.

Nauchno-Praktichesky Kommentarii k Ugolovno-Protsessualnomy Kodeksu RSFSR (Scientific-Practical Commentary on the RSFSR Criminal Procedure Code), by Aleksandrov, G. N., Anashkin, G. Z., Grun, A. Ya., Minkovsky, G. M., Novikov, S. G., Perlov, I. D., Raginsky, M. Yu., ed. Boldyrev, V. A., State Publishing House of Juridical Literature, Moscow, 1963.

Neishtadt, T. E., *Sovetsky Advokat* (The Soviet Defence Lawyer), Society for the Dissemination of Political and Scientific Knowledge of the RSFSR, Moscow, 1958.

Novoye Ugolovnoye Zakonodatelstvo RSFSR—Materialy Nauchnoi Sessii (New RSFSR Criminal Legislation—Proceedings of a Scientific Session), All-Union Institute of Juridical Science, State Publishing House of Juridical Literature, Moscow, 1961.

Novy Mir (New World), periodical, organ of the USSR Writers' Union.

Oktyabr (October), periodical, organ of the RSFSR Writers' Union.

Osobo-Opasnye Gosudarstvennye Prestupleniya (Specially Dangerous State Crimes), by Bogatikov, D. I., Bushuev, I. A., Ignatov, A. N., Kurlyandsky, V. I., Mikhailov, M. P., and Smirnov, E. A., ed. Kurlyandsky and Mikhailov, State Publishing House of Juridical Literature, Moscow, 1963.

Ostroumov, S. S., *Sovetskaya Sudebnaya Statistika* (Soviet Judicial Statistics), Moscow University Publishing House, 1962.

Partiinaya Zhizn (Party Life), periodical, organ of the Central Committee of the Communist Party of the Soviet Union.

Perlov, I. D., *Kak Ustroyen Sud, Prokuratura i Advokatura v SSSR* (How the Courts, the Prosecutor's Office and the Defence Lawyers are Organised in the USSR), 'Knowledge' Publishing House, Moscow, 1964.

Perlov, I. D., *Organizatsiya Raboty Narodnogo Suda* (Organisation of Work of the People's Court), State Publishing House of Juridical Literature, Moscow, 1950.

Perlov, I. D., *Organizatsiya Raboty Sovetskogo Suda* (Organisation of Work of the Soviet Court), State Publishing House of Juridical Literature, Moscow, 1953.

Perlov, I. D., *Sudebnoye Sledstviye v Sovetskom Ugolovnom Protsesse* (Court Proceedings in Soviet Criminal Trial), State Publishing House of Juridical Literature, Moscow, 1955.

Piontkovsky, A. A., *Ucheniye o Prestuplenii po Sovetskomu Ugolovnomu Pravu* (The Study of Crime in Soviet Criminal Law), State Publishing House of Juridical Literature, Moscow, 1964.

Piontkovsky, A. A., and Menshagin, V. D., *Kurs Sovetskogo Ugolovnogo Prava—Osobennaya Chast* (A Course of Soviet Criminal Law—Special Section), State Publishing House of Juridical Literature, Moscow, 1955.

Politicheskoye Samoobrazovaniye (Political Self-education), periodical, organ of the Central Committee of the Communist Party of the Soviet Union.

Pravda (Truth), newspaper, organ of the Central Committee of the Communist Party of the Soviet Union.

Pravda Ukrainy (Truth of the Ukraine), newspaper, organ of the Central Committee of the Communist Party of the Ukraine and of the Supreme Soviet and Council of Ministers of the Ukrainian SSR.

Pravda Vostoka (Truth of the East), newspaper, organ of the Central Committee of the Communist Party of Uzbekistan and of the Supreme Soviet of the Uzbek SSR.

Pravovye Garantii Zakonnosti v SSSR (Legal Guarantees of Legality in the USSR), ed. Strogovich, M. S., USSR Academy of Sciences Publishing House, Moscow, 1962.

Problemy Iskoreniya Prestupnosti (Problems of Eradicating Criminality), edited V. N. Kudryavtsev, N. A. Yakubovich, V. M. Nikolaichik, A. A. Gertsenzon, G. A. Zlobin, V. G. Tanasevich, A. M. Yakovlev, 'Juridical Literature' Publishing House, Moscow, 1965.

Raginsky, M. Yu., *Vospitatelnaya Rol Sovetskogo Suda* (The Educative Rôle of the Soviet Court), State Publishing House of Juridical Science, Moscow, 1959.

Rakhunov, R. D., *Peresmotr Prigovorov i Opredelenii v Prezidiumakh Sudov* (The Reviewing of Verdicts and Decisions in Court Presidiums), State Publishing House of Juridical Literature, Moscow, 1956.

Rakhunov, R. D., *Uchastniki Ugolovno-Protsessualnoi Deyatelnosti po Sovetskomu Pravu* (Parties to Criminal Procedure in Soviet Law), State Publishing House of Juridical Literature, Moscow, 1961.

Rivlin, A. L., *Peresmotr Prigovorov v SSSR* (The Reviewing of Verdicts in the USSR), State Publishing House of Juridical Literature, Moscow, 1958.

RSFSR Laws:

1917–38: *Sobranie Ukazoneniy i Rasporyazheniy Raboche-Krestyanskogo Pravitelstva Rossiyskoy Sovetskoy Respubliki* (Collection of Statutes and Orders of the Worker-Peasant Government of the Russian Soviet Federative Socialist Republic), People's Commissariat of Justice of the RSFSR, Moscow.

1943– : *Sobranie Postanovleniy i Rasporyazheniy Pravitelstva Rossiyskoy Sovetskoy Federativnoy Sotsialisticheskoy Respubliki* (Collection of Decrees and Orders of the Government of the Russian Soviet Federative Socialist Republic), People's Commissariat (Ministry from April, 1946) of Justice of the RSFSR, then (from March, 1947) Administration of Affairs of the Council of Ministers of the RSFSR, Moscow.

Sakharov, A. B., *O Lichosti Prestupnika i Prichinakh Prestupnosti v SSSR* (On the Character of the Criminal and the Causes of Crime in the USSR), State Publishing House of Juridical Literature, Moscow, 1961.

Savitsky, V. M., and Rozenbaum, Yu. A., *Novoye Zakonodatelstvo v Oblasti Ugolovnogo Prava, Sudoustroistva i Ugolovnogo Sudoproizvodstva* (New Legislation in the Fields of Criminal Law, the Judicial System and Criminal Judicial Procedure), Moscow, 1959.

Sbornik Deistvuyushchikh Postanovlenii Plenuma Verkhovnogo Suda SSSR, 1924–1957 (Collection of Current Decisions of the Plenum of the Supreme Court of the USSR, 1924–1957), edited N. K. Morozov, State Publishing House of Juridical Literature, Moscow, 1958.

Shargorodsky, M., *Voprosy Obshchey Chasti Ugolovnogo Prava* (Questions of the General Section of Criminal Law), Leningrad University Publishing House, Leningrad, 1955.

Shebanov, A. F., *Normy Sovetskogo Sotsialisticheskogo Prava* (Norms of Soviet Socialist Law), Moscow University Publishing House, Moscow, 1956.

Sladkov, K. S., *Poryadok Vyborov Raionnykh (Gorodskikh) Narodnykh Sudov* (The Procedure for Elections to District [Town] People's Courts), 'Juridical Literature' Publishing House, Moscow, 1965.

Sokolov, Yu. A., *Uchastiye Trudyashchikhsya v Okhrane Sovetskogo Obshchestvennogo Poryadka* (Workers' Participation in the Protection of Soviet Public Order), State Publishing House of Juridical Literature, Moscow, 1962.

Solovyev, D. D., *Voprosy Primeneniya Nakazaniya po Sovetskomu Ugolovnomu Pravu* (Questions of the Application of Punishment in Soviet Criminal Law), State Publishing House of Juridical Literature, Moscow, 1958.

Sorok Let Sovetskogo Prava, 1917–1957, tom 2—Period Sotsializma (Forty Years of Soviet Law, 1917–1957, volume 2—The Period of Socialism), edited M. D. Shargorodsky, Leningrad University Publishing House, Leningrad, 1957.

Sotsialisticheskaya Zakonnost (Socialist Legality), periodical, organ of the Prosecutor's Office of the USSR and the USSR Supreme Court.

Sovetskaya Kirgiziya (Soviet Kirgizia), newspaper, organ of the Central Committee of the Communist Party of Kirgizia and of the Supreme Soviet and the Council of Ministers of the Kirgiz SSR.

Sovetskaya Rossiya (Soviet Russia), newspaper, organ of the Central Committee of the CPSU.

Sovetskaya Yustitsiya (Soviet Justice), periodical, organ of the Supreme Court of the RSFSR and of the Juridical Commission attached to the RSFSR Council of Ministers.

Sovetskoye Gosudarstvo i Pravo (Soviet State and Law), periodical, organ of the Institute of State and Law of the USSR Academy of Sciences.

Sovetskoye Ugolovnoye Pravo—Osobennaya Chast (Soviet Criminal Law—Special Section), edited B. S. Utevsky, State Publishing House of Juridical Literature, Moscow, 1958.

Sovetsky Ugolovny Protsess (Soviet Criminal Trial), edited D. S. Karev, State Publishing House of Juridical Literature, Moscow, 1953.

Stalin, *Problems of Leninism*, translated from 11th Russian edition, Foreign Languages Publishing House, Moscow, 1953.

Stalin, *Works*, volumes 1–13, Foreign Languages Publishing House, Moscow, 1952–55.

Tadevosyan, V. S., *Prokurorsky Nadzor v SSSR* (Supervision by the Prosecutor in the USSR), State Publishing House of Juridical Literature, Moscow, 1956.

Tkachenko, Yu. G., *Normy Sovetskogo Sotsialisticheskogo Prava i ikh Primenenie* (Norms of Soviet Socialist Law and the Application of Them), State Publishing House of Juridical Literature, Moscow, 1955.

Tovarishcheskiye Sudy (Comrades' Courts), compiler A. B. Sakharov, 'Knowledge' Publishing House, Moscow, 1966.

Trud (Labour), newspaper, organ of the All-Union Central Council of Trade Unions.

Trusov, A. I., *Osnovy Teorii Sudebnykh Dokazatelstv* (Foundations of the Theory of Court Evidence), State Publishing House of Juridical Literature, Moscow, 1960.

Turetsky, M. V., *Osobo Opasnye Gosudarstvennye Prestupleniya* (Specially Dangerous State Crimes), Moscow University Publishing House, 1965.

Ugolovnoye Pravo, Chast Osobennaya (Criminal Law, Special Section), edited B. V. Zdravomyslov, C. G. Kelina, Sh. C. Rashkovskaya, M. A. Shneider, 'Juridical Literature' Publishing House, Moscow, 1966.

Ugolovnoye Zakonodatelstvo Soyuza SSR i Soyuznykh Respublik (Criminal Legislation of the USSR and the Union Republics), vols. 1–2, State Publishing House of Juridical Literature, Moscow, 1963.

USSR Laws:

1924–38: *Sobranie Zakonov i Rasporyazheniy Raboche-Krestyanskogo Pravitelstva Soyuza Sovetskikh Sotsialisticheskikh Respublik* (Collection of Laws and Orders of the Worker–Peasant Government of the Union of Soviet Socialist Republics), Administration of Affairs of the Council of People's Commissars of the USSR, Moscow.

1938–49: *Sobranie Postanovleniy i Rasporyazheniy Pravitelstva Soyuza Sovetskikh Sotsialisticheskikh Respublik* (Collection of Decrees and Orders of the Government of the Union of Soviet Socialist Republics), Administration of Affairs of the Council of People's Commissars (Ministers from April, 1946) of the USSR, Moscow.

Vechernyaya Moskva (Evening Moscow), newspaper, organ of the Moscow City Committee of the Communist Party of the Soviet Union and of the Moscow Soviet.

Vedomosti Verkhovnogo Soveta RSFSR (Gazette of the RSFSR Supreme Soviet), periodical, organ of the Supreme Soviet of the RSFSR.

Vedomosti Verkhovnogo Soveta SSSR (Gazette of the USSR Supreme Soviet), periodical, organ of the Supreme Soviet of the USSR.

Verchenko, A. Ya., *Dvadtsat Vtoroi Syezd KPSS i Dalneisheye Ukrepleniye Sotsialisticheskoi Zakonnosti v SSSR* (The Twenty-Second Congress of the CPSU and the Further Strengthening of Socialist Legality in the USSR), Publishing House of the Higher Party School and the Academy of Social Sciences of the CCCPSU, Moscow, 1963.

Vestnik Moskovskogo Universiteta (The Herald of Moscow University), periodical, Moscow University Publishing House. (The references are to the Law Series.)

Voprosy Kodifikatsii Sovetskogo Prava (Questions of the Codification of Soviet Law), edited D. A. Kerimov, Leningrad University Publishing House, 1957.

[151]

Voprosy Sudoproizvodstva i Sudoustroistva v Novom Zakonodatel-stve Soyuza SSR (Questions of Judicial Proceedings and the Judicial System in New USSR Legislation), edited S. A. Golunsky, State Publishing House of Juridical Literature, Moscow, 1959.

Vorozheikin, E. M., *Kratky Spravochnik Predsedatelya i Chlena Tovarishcheskogo Suda* (A Short Handbook for the Chairman and Members of a Comrades' Court), All-Union Central Council of Trade Unions, Profizdat Publishing House, Moscow, 1965.

Vyshinsky, A. Ya., *Sudoustroistvo v SSSR* (The Judicial System in the USSR), 3rd edition, Moscow, 1936.

Yudelson, K. S., *Polozheniye o Tovarishcheskikh Sudakh* (Regulatory Order on Comrades' Courts), State Publishing House of Juridical Literature, Moscow, 1962.

Yuridichesky Slovar (Juridical Dictionary), State Publishing House of Juridical Literature, Moscow, 1953.

Zarya Vostoka (Dawn of the East), newspaper, organ of the Central Committee of the Communist Party of Georgia and of the Supreme Soviet and Council of Ministers of the Georgian SSR.

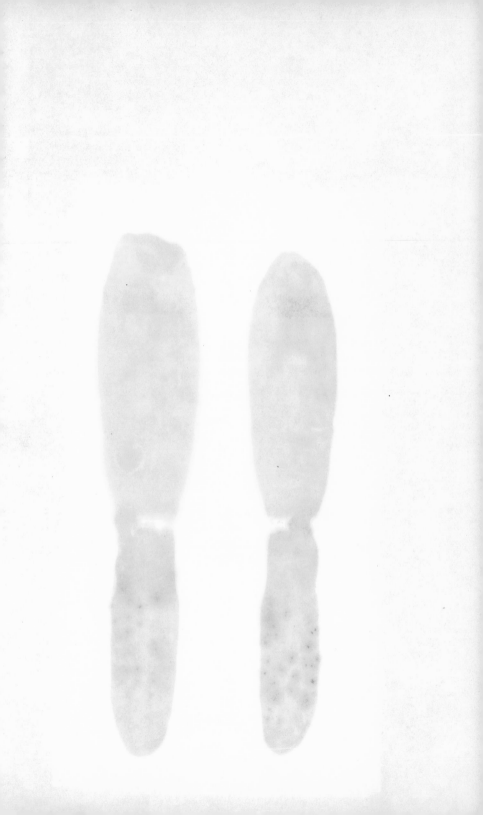

DATE DUE